MESHIAGARE
めしあがれ

A Culinary Journey through Advanced Japanese
食文化で学ぶ上級日本語

畑佐一味・福留奈美 [著]
Hatasa Kazumi, Fukutome Nami

くろしお出版

はじめに

　人間は調理をする唯一の動物です。私たちの祖先は食材を調理することで、食べられるものの幅を広げ、さらに「おいしく食べる」ことを学び、それを喜びと感じ、工夫するようになりました。その結果、世界各地で特有の食文化を作り出しました。

　寿司が世界化した SUSHI が牽引車となり、日本の料理が海外で注目されるようになりました。さらに、2013 年には「和食」がユネスコ無形文化遺産に登録され、世界的にも評価されました。現在、外国人があげる日本訪問の理由第一位は「日本での食体験」です。（日本政府観光局）

　本書は日本の食文化をテーマに据えた内容中心の日本語教材です。日本の食文化の多様な面を紹介し、理解を深めてもらうことを目的としています。日本食の基本となる出汁やうま味はもとより、和食、洋食、弁当、郷土料理、B級グルメ、ラーメンや給食、箸、食のタブーなど、日本の食文化の様々なトピックを通し、歴史的な背景や変遷、日本文化や社会問題を理解し、更に学習者（読者）自身の食の倫理観や価値観についても考えたり、リサーチをするなど活動型の構成となっています。

　また、調理体験も本書を使っていただく上で大切な活動と位置づけ、簡単においしく作れる人気の日本食レシピを各章で紹介しています。日本国外でも調達しやすい食材と調味料に配慮し、レシピもわかりやすい表現を用いて説明してあります（料理の専門的な用語は巻末で解説）。是非、学習者と一緒に料理を作るという活動を授業計画の中に組み込んで頂きたいと思います。また、多様な日本語レベルの学習者に対応するために、本文とレシピに英語翻訳を用意しています。適宜利用することで、内容（コンテント）の理解に焦点を当てた授業が可能になります。また、英語で日本の食文化について学びたい方や英語学習者にもご利用いただけます。ウェブサイト「めしあがれウェブ」では、本書と関連した写真や動画、紹介しきれなかった内容やリサーチに役立つ追加情報を提供しています。

　本書を通して、日本語学習者や日本に興味のある方々が、日本の食文化への理解を深め、料理体験をするという楽しい活動が展開されることを期待します。

　本書を執筆するための資料集めの段階で博報堂教育財団日本研究フェローシップのご支援を頂いたことに感謝いたします。また、出版に際して、編集を担当してくださったくろしお出版市川麻里子様のご苦労に感謝します。

2021 年春　著者

目　次 ● CONTETS

第1章　日本の食文化の特徴　　　　10
　　column　味に関することば

第2章　関東と関西の料理の違い　　14
　　column　「くだらない」の意味と食べ物

第3章　出汁とうま味　　　　　　　19
　　column　食感のことば

第4章　寿司　　　　　　　　　　　24
　　column　「さかな」の語源

第5章　洋食のはじまり　　　　　　29
　　column　パン粉と生パン粉

第6章　米　　　　　　　　　　　　34
　　column　「落とし蓋」ってどんな蓋？

第7章　箸　　　　　　　　　　　　38
　　column　きれいな箸の持ち方

第8章　和食の麺（うどん・蕎麦）　42
　　column　麺の「コシ」ってなに？

第9章　弁当と駅弁　　　　　　　　47
　　column　海苔について

第10章　給食　　　　　　　　　　　52
　　column　1カップの謎

第11章　郷土料理とB級ご当地グルメ　57
　　column　わんこ蕎麦

第12章　食文化と価値観　　　　　　61
　　column　天ぷらの衣ってなに？

第13章　ラーメン　　　　　　　　　66
　　column　ラーメンのことば

第14章　うなぎ（鰻）　　　　　　　71
　　column　関西と関東の蒲焼きの違い

第15章　お好み焼き　　　　　　　　76
　　column　「ねかす」って寝かす？

レシピ

天ぷら　　　　　　　　　13

月見蕎麦　　　　　　　　18

だし巻き卵　　　　　　　23

サーモンちらし寿司　　　28

とんかつ　　　　　　　　33

炊き込みご飯　　　　　　37

味噌汁　　　　　　　　　41

手打ちうどん　　　　　　46

おにぎり　　　　　　　　51

ビーフカレーライス　　　56

唐揚げ　　　　　　　　　60

肉じゃが　　　　　　　　65

煮たまご入りラーメン　　70

親子丼　　　　　　　　　75

お好み焼き　　　　　　　80

Chapter 1	Japanese Food Culture	82
Chapter 2	Kanto and Kansai Regional Cuisine - A Comparison	85
Chapter 3	Dashi and Umami	89
Chapter 4	Sushi	93
Chapter 5	The Origin of Yoshoku	97
Chapter 6	Rice	101
Chapter 7	Chopsticks	104
Chapter 8	Japanese Noodles–Udon and Soba	107
Chapter 9	Lunch Boxes - Bento and Ekiben	111
Chapter 10	School Lunch	115
Chapter 11	Regional Cuisine and B-Class Gourmet Cuisine	119
Chapter 12	Food Culture and Values	122
Chapter 13	Ramen	126
Chapter 14	Eel	130
Chapter 15	Okonomiyaki	134

● 料理のことば 138

● 参考文献 141

Tempura	84
Tsukimi Moon-Viewing Soba in Kanto-style Soup	88
Dashi-maki Tamago (Rolled Omelet)	92
Samon Chirashi-zushi (Salmon Scattered Sushi)	96
Tonkatsu (Breaded Pork Cutlet)	100
Tori Gomoku Meshi (Rice Cooked with Chicken and Vegetables)	103
Miso Soup	106
Homemade Udon Noodles	110
Onigiri (Rice Balls)	114
Kare Raisu (Beef Curry with Rice)	118
Karaage (Fried Chicken)	121
Nikujaga (Meat and Potatoes)	125
Ramen noodles with *Nitamago* Seasoned boiled eggs	129
Oyako-don (Chicken and Egg Bowl)	133
Okonomiyaki (Savory Pancake)	137

本書の対象者

▶ 上級レベル（JLPT N1 〜 N2 程度）の日本語学習者であればスムーズに学習できますが、中上級（JLPT N2 〜 N3 程度）の学習者でも、語彙を確認しながら学習できます。

▶ ルビは JLPT N2 相当以上の漢字語彙、固有名詞に付加。

各章の構成

▶本文	各章のテーマを反映した読み物
▶内容質問	本文の内容の基本的な理解をチェックするための質問 （解答は「めしあがれウェブ」）
▶発展問題	本文の内容を踏まえ、発展させたプロジェクト（リサーチ、発表） 学習者自身の意見を求める質問、グループ活動
▶食のひとくちメモ	ちょっとおもしろい食の言葉や表現、料理の豆知識など
▶レシピ	簡単で作りやすく、おいしい日本食のレシピの紹介
▶英語翻訳	本文とレシピの全文英語翻訳

> **めしあがれウェブ**
> ● 本文語彙リスト ● オリジナル写真（料理など）● レシピ動画
> ● リンク紹介（YouTube などの動画、無料単語帳アプリ）
> ● 発展問題のための追加資料

勉強の仕方

▶ 本書は上級（中上級でも可）の日本語クラスでも、自習でも楽しく学べます。

▶ 本文を読み、内容質問で理解を深め、発展問題でプロジェクト活動をしましょう。

▶ 本文は文法的に難しくないですが、これまでの日本語学習では習わなかった料理や食に関連した語彙が多く含まれています。はじめに「単語リスト（「めしあがれウェブ」参照）」で、単語の練習をしてから本文を読むと理解が深まります。また、英語がわかる人は、英語訳を先に読み、内容理解をした上で日本語を読むのもいいでしょう。

▶ 本文の理解には日本の歴史の知識が助けになります。さらに、自分の国の歴史と日本の歴史を重ね合わせたり対比したりできると理解が進みます。

▶「めしあがれウェブ」では本文の内容をさらに深め、展開させる情報をたくさん紹介しています。発展問題で調査したりレポートする際に役立ちます。

▶ レシピにしたがって実際に料理をすることは、内容を理解する上でも大切です。是非体験してみてください。

料理の基本

本書のレシピでは、分量をミリリットル（ml）、グラム（g）、センチメートル（cm）で、温度を摂氏（度／℃）で示しています。

▶ 計量カップ：国によって大きさが違います。計量カップを使う場合は、各自で確認してください。

1 カップ量の違い	
日本	1 カップ = 200ml
アメリカ	1 カップ＝約 240ml（8oz）
イギリス、カナダ、オーストラリア、ニュージーランドなど	1 カップ＝約 250ml（8oz）

▶ 計量スプーン：各国同じです。容量(ml) と重量(g) は、計る材料によって違います。

容量	重量（g）
大さじ 1 = 15ml	しょうゆ・みりん・みそ 18g、水・酒・酢 15g、油 12g、塩（精製塩 18g、粗塩 15g）、上白糖・薄力粉・強力粉 9g
小さじ 1 = 5ml	しょうゆ・みりん・みそ 6g、水・酒・酢 5g、油 4g、塩（精製塩 6g、粗塩 5g）、上白糖・薄力粉・強力粉 3g

▶ 温度：油やオーブンの温度は、日本では摂氏（℃）で表しますが、アメリカでは華氏（°F）で表します。

170℃ = 340°F	180℃ = 360°F

▶ コンロ：ガスコンロと電気コンロは、温まる速さや消したあとの冷める速さが違うので、適宜調整してください。日本はガスコンロが多いです。

▶ 水：国によって、水の硬度（hardness）が違います。硬度によって、スープや煮物などの味が変わることがあります。日本の水は基本的に硬度が低い軟水です。出汁のおいしさにこだわりたい時には、硬度の低い（硬度 60mg/ℓ 以下）軟水のミネラルウォーターを利用するといいでしょう。

▶ 食材の調達：海外で日本食関係の食材を調達する場合、アジア食品店を利用することが一番多いです。日本の食材の他、中国、韓国、インド、タイ、ベトナムなどの食材も売っています。

教師の皆様へ

教え方のヒントを「めしあがれウェブ」で紹介しています。

参考にしてください。　http://one-taste.org/meshiagare/

Target Audience for This Text

▶ Advanced Japanese learners (JLPT N1-N2) will be able to follow the content well. This text is also appropriate for intermediate Japanese learners (JLPTN2-N3) who may wish to reference vocabulary words as they follow along.

▶ Kanji readings are provided for vocabulary from JLPT N2 level and above as well as for proper nouns.

Chapter Composition

▶ Main Text	Material related to each chapter theme
▶ Content Questions	Questions checking readers' basic understanding of the text (answers available on Meshiagare Web)
▶ Development Questions	Suggestions for further projects (research, presentations), questions seeking readers' opinions, and group work based on the text.
▶ Bite-sized Memos	Interesting food-related terms and phrases and cooking trivia.
▶ Recipes	Delicious, easy-to-make Japanese recipes
▶ English Translation	Full English translation of the main text and recipes

Meshiagare Web

● Main text vocabulary lists ● Photos of foods and other items ● Recipe videos
● Useful links (for YouTube videos and free vocabulary flash card apps)
● Additional resources for development questions

Study Methods

▶ This text is intended to make Japanese language learning fun either in classroom settings (for advanced or intermediate Japanese) or during self-study.

▶ First read the text. Next, deepen your understanding through the content questions. And lastly, try working on a project suggestion from the development questions section.

▶ This text is not grammatically difficult, however, it does include many cooking and food-related vocabulary words that may not have been covered in previous Japanese language studies. We recommend first reviewing the "Vocabulary Lists" available on Meshiagare Web and practicing the terms prior to reading the main text. For English speakers, it may help to read the English text first to aid comprehension before proceeding to the Japanese text.

▶ Some knowledge of Japanese history is helpful in understanding this text, and being able to layer the history of your own country with that of Japan's will also aid understanding.

▶ Meshiagare Web contains a lot of information to deepen understanding of the main text content. It also contains resources that will be helpful when writing research reports as suggested in the development questions.

▶ It is important to gain first-hand understanding of the content by cooking the recipes in this text. Please give them a try!

Cooking Basics

The recipes in this text show quantities in milliliters (**ml**), grams (**g**), and centimeters (**cm**), and temperatures are shown in Celsius (**°C**).

▶ **Measuring Cups** : The volume in a cup varies by country. When using a measuring cup, please be sure to double-check the required quantity.

Different Meanings for 1 Cup
Japan 1 cup = 200 ml
USA 1 cup = approx. 240 ml (8 oz)
UK, Canada, Australia, New Zealand 1 cup = approx. 250 ml (8 oz)

▶ **Measuring Spoons** : Same size in every country. The volume or weight varies by ingredient.

Volume	Weight (g)
1 tablespoon = 15 ml	Soy sauce, mirin, miso = 18 g; water, sake, vinegar = 15 g; oil = 12 g; salt (refined salt 18 g, coarse salt 15 g); superfine sugar, cake flour, bread flour = 9 g
1 teaspoon = 5 ml	Soy sauce, mirin, miso = 6 g; water, sake, vinegar = 5 g; oil = 4 g; salt (refined salt 6 g, coarse salt 5 g); superfine sugar, cake flour, bread flour = 3 g

▶ **Temperature** : In Japan, oven and oil temperatures are shown in Celsius (**°C**), whereas in the United States they are shown in Fahrenheit (**°F**).

170°C = 340°F	180°C = 360°F

▶ **Stovetop** : The speed at which gas and electric stovetops heat up and cool down is very different, so please adjust accordingly. In Japan, most people use gas stovetops.

▶ **Water** : Water hardness varies by country and this can affect the flavor of soups and simmered dishes. In Japan, water is typically quite soft. When you wish to get the best flavor from your dashi, try using store-bought soft mineral water (with hardness below 60 mg/ liter).

▶ **Finding Ingredients** : When searching for Japanese ingredients overseas, it is best to look in Asian food stores where they sell Japanese ingredients in addition to items from China, Korea, India, Thailand, Vietnam, and other countries of Asia.

For Teachers

Please reference Meshiagare Web for tips on teaching with this text.

http://one-taste.org/meshiagare/

日本の食文化の特徴

　日本は北緯45°から20°(アメリカ大陸では、メイン州からフロリダ州、ヨーロッパでは、北イタリアからアフリカのモロッコに当たる)に位置しており、北海道、本州、四国、九州の四つの島を中心に、6,500以上の島からなります。日本の大部分は温帯に属していて四季がはっきりしていますが、北海道は亜寒帯、沖縄は亜熱帯に属しています。国土の約75%は山地で、中央には3,000メートル級の高い山脈があり、河川も多く、水量が豊富で、水質もいいです。さらに、近海を暖流と寒流が流れていて、世界でも有数の豊かな漁場が多くあります。ですから、日本では新鮮な魚介類、野菜、肉などの食材が豊富で、海と山の幸の両方を味わうことができるのです。日本人はこのような恵まれた気候と風土を利用して、多彩な食材を調達し、料理に使ってきました。その結果生まれた日本の食文化には以下のような特徴があります。

　第一に、「素材の味を引き立たせる」という基本理念があります。料理人は素材にあまり手を加えず、素材本来の香りや味、食感などを最大限に引き出す努力をします。刺身はその代表的なものです。和食では魚が新鮮なら、まず生で食べることを選びます。そして、鮮度が落ちてくると、火を通して焼き物や煮物といった料理にします。もちろん、古い時代には実際に魚を生で食べられたのは海岸の近くにいた人達に限られていましたが、山に住む人も「魚は刺身が一番おいしい」と考えていたようです。そして、このように生食の伝統が強い日本では、生鮮食品の鮮度を保つための技術も発達し、消費者も食材の鮮度には敏感です。日本の食の安全性が世界的に認識されている一つの理由と言えるかもしれません。

　第二に、日本には「食べる物で季節の変化を感じる」という習慣があります。四季の区別がはっきりしている日本では季節の変化に伴って、食材も変化します。さらに、年中行事や祭りと食材が関連づけられています。一年の中で特定の魚や

野菜がおいしくなる時期をその食材の「旬」
と呼びます。例えば、ブリという魚の旬は冬
で、漁獲量が多く、味もおいしくなります。
冬のブリは「寒ブリ」と呼ばれます。ブリが
スーパーで見かけられるようになると、日本
人は冬の訪れを感じます。また、10月は栗が
旬です。10月になると栗を使った料理がたくさん見られるようになり、栗を使っ
た和菓子や洋菓子が店に並びます。冷凍・冷蔵技術の発達で現在は旬が感じづら
くなっていますが、会席料理のような和食のコース料理は必ず旬を意識して食材
が選ばれます。また、フランス料理やイタリア料理のレストランでも季節に合っ
た旬の食材を使った料理を出しています。「旬」を意識して食材を見ると日本の食
生活をより深く楽しめるようになります。

　第三に、「食に対する柔軟性」が挙げられます。日本人は外国の衣食住の習慣な
どをあまり抵抗なく生活に取り入れる傾向があります。例えば、一般家庭で和風、
洋風、中華やその他のエスニック料理など、異なる国々の料理を日常的に作って
います。そして、それらはしばしば同じ食卓の上に登場します。日本人は伝統を
重んじますが、新しいものに順応もします。明治維新の時に見られたように、急
激な西洋化の波の中からでもとんかつやカレーライスなど日本化された西洋料理
が生み出され、それらは「洋食」と呼ばれるようになりました。

　最後に、「米の重要性」を日本の食文化の特徴として挙げます。米は約三千年ほ
ど前にアジア大陸から日本に伝わったとされ、その後稲作が始められました。戦
後の食の欧米化に伴い、昔に比べると米の消費量は減ってはいますが、現在でも
大切な主食です。また、米は歴史の中で単なる食材以上の役割を果たしてきまし
た。古くは、米は富を意味し、神への供物や租税として使われたり、武士の給料
としても使われていました。現代の日本でも米
は単なる農作物以上の地位を占め、米から作ら
れる餅や酒、炊いた飯や稲穂などが色々な儀式
や祭事でも頻繁に使われています。そして、稲
作は農業政策的にも保護されています。

●内容質問

1　日本は食材が豊かな国です。それはどうしてですか。

2　日本の食文化の特徴を説明して下さい。

3　「旬」を説明して下さい。

4　「米」はどうして特別な作物として扱われるようになったのですか。

●発展問題

1　皆さんの国はどのような気候帯（climate zone）にありますか。

2　皆さんの国ではどのような食材がとれますか。

3　皆さんの国の食材や料理で季節と結びついているものはありますか。

4　皆さんの国の料理の特徴は何ですか。

味に関することば

1）人が舌で感じる味のことばは「甘い」、「しょっぱい・しおからい」、「にがい」、「すっぱい」、そして「うま味がある」の五つです。

・このトマト、**甘くて**、おいしいですね。

・塩を入れすぎて、**しょっぱくなって／しおからくなって**しまったね。

・チョコレートもカカオ 70% 以上になると、**にがい**です。

・レモンはそれだけでは**すっぱい**から、少し砂糖を入れるといいですよ。

・この味噌汁は、出汁の**うま味がきいて**ておいしいですね。

2）「甘ずっぱい」や「甘辛」など味が混ざった時のことばもあります。

・砂糖を少しいれると、そのジュースは**甘ずっぱく**なっておいしいですよ。

・この団子の**甘辛**の味が大好きです。（醤油と砂糖を混ぜた味）

3）「辛い (spicy)」と「渋い (astringent)」は味ではなく、「刺激」と認識されています。

・**辛い**カレーを食べると、汗がたくさん出ます。

・煎茶は熱湯でいれると、**渋く**なります。

 天ぷら

天ぷら衣の作り方と揚げ方のコツがわかれば、いろいろな季節の食材を天種にして楽しめます。天つゆだけでなく、抹茶塩やこだわりの塩をつけて食べてもおいしいです。

●材料（2人分）

<天種>

殻付きエビ	2~4尾
かぼちゃ	薄切り4枚
なす	小1本
しいたけ	小2枚
さやいんげん	2-4本
大葉	2枚
揚げ油	適宜

<天ぷら衣>

溶き卵	大さじ1
冷水	100ml
薄力粉	120ml（約70g）

<天つゆ>

水	200ml
和風顆粒だし	小さじ1/4
こいくち醤油、みりん	各大さじ1
大根おろし	大さじ3

●作り方

1 エビは殻をむき、尾の先端を切り落とし、身は切り込みを入れて長くまっすぐに整える。かぼちゃは薄切りに、なすは4等分して切り込みを入れ、しいたけは軸を切り、上に十字の切り込みを入れる。さやいんげんは半分に切る。大葉は洗って水気をきっておく。

2 天つゆの材料を小鍋に入れて沸かす。大根はすりおろして水気をきっておく。

3 溶き卵に冷水（※水に氷を入れて冷たくし、氷を抜いた水）を混ぜ合わせる。水分と同量（※ここでは120ml程度）の薄力粉をザルでふるいながら加え、菜箸でたたくようにかき混ぜ、粉が少し残るくらいにして天ぷら衣を作る。

4 深めのフライパンに揚げ油を7分目くらいまで入れ、火にかける。170℃まで熱する。

5 天種に薄力粉（分量外）を軽くまぶしてから、天ぷら衣をつけて油に入れて揚げる。油から取り出す直前に、油の温度を180℃くらいに上げるとからりと揚がる。

料理のことば 溶き卵, 切り込み, 分量外, まぶす, からりと ➡ p.138

 TIPS
・天種には、白身魚切り身、イカ、鶏肉、れんこん、玉ねぎ、さつまいも、アスパラガス、ズッキーニ、海苔、キノコ各種などもおすすめ。
・天ぷら衣は卵1個に対して200~400mlの冷水を加えます。冷水の割合を少なくすると衣はやわらかめ、多いと衣はサクッとかために揚がります。
・市販の麺つゆを使えば、薄めるだけで天つゆを作ることができます。

第2章 関東と関西の料理の違い

　一つの国の中でも育った所が少し違うだけで文化的な地域差が生まれます。それは自分の地域に対するプライドや他の地域に対する競争心という形で現れます。アメリカなら北部と南部、あるいは東海岸、西海岸、オーストラリアならビクトリア州とクイーンズランド州、イギリスならそれぞれの四つの地域など、どの国でも地域差があります。中国も北部と南部では食材も調味料も大きく違います。日本では東京を中心とした関東と大阪を中心とした関西という分け方がよく使われ、その違いは食文化にも顕著に現れています。

　関東と関西の食文化の違いを最もよく表しているのは「出汁」と「醤油」でしょう。現在はどちらも使うようになりましたが、歴史的には、関西は昆布出汁が中心で、関東はかつお出汁が中心でした。昆布は北の冷たい海で育つ海藻です。室町時代から江戸時代の始

昆布　　　かつお節

めまでは、北海道で採れた昆布を日本海を通る船で、現在の福井県に輸送し、その後、琵琶湖を通り最後は陸路で京都まで運びました。その結果、京都では昆布から取った出汁を使った京料理の味が確立していきました。昆布出汁は味がまろやかなので、京料理もその味を生かした味付けが施されています。一方、カツオは太平洋で獲れる魚で、その身を加工したかつお節が太平洋側で作られるようになり、江戸で広まっていきました。かつお出汁は昆布出汁に比べると風味が強いのが特徴です。その後は全国で両方の出汁が使われるようになっていきました。現在では「合わせ出汁」といって、昆布とかつお節の両方から出汁をとってうま味を強調したものもよく使われます。

　醤油は日本の食生活にとって最も大切な発酵調味料です。大豆と小麦に種麹（コウジカビの胞子）を加えて麹を作り、塩水を加えて仕込み、6ヶ月から1年以上寝かせます。すると、コウジカビ、酵母、乳酸菌など

醤油

の働きで、発酵が進み、醤油ができます。大豆と小麦で作る醤油だけでなく、大豆100%で作る醤油もあります。

　醤油の原形は8世紀に中国から伝えられ、その後、日本独自の発酵調味料としてまず味噌が発達しました。味噌を作る行程の途中で出る汁を取り出したものが醤油のはじまりです。これが、現在の「たまり醤油」と呼ばれるものの原形です。

　17世紀の江戸時代初期に兵庫県(関西)と千葉県(関東)で少し違った二種類の醤油が作られるようになりました。醤油は最初関西での生産量が多く、関東に運ばれていましたが、江戸時代後期には関東でも生産量が増えました。どちらも大豆と小麦の麹を塩水と混ぜて発酵させて作りますが、関西の醤油は色が薄く、あっさりとした風味に仕上げたので「うすくち醤油」と呼ばれました。一方、関東の醤油は色が濃く、醤油の風味が強かったので「こいくち醤油」と呼ばれるようになりました。ただし、醤油の濃い薄いはあくまでも色の濃淡で、塩分はどちらもあまり変わりません。

うすくち醤油　　こいくち醤油

　この違いは現在でも関西と関東の料理の違いに見ることができます。関西では瀬戸内海で獲れる近海物の魚が多く食べられ、肉質は白身で味が淡白なものが中心でした。その代表的なものはタイです。そのような食材をうすくち醤油と昆布出汁で調理すると素材の味を生かした色も綺麗な料理に仕上がります。一方、関東の魚はマグロやカツオなど太平洋で獲れる赤身の魚が中心でした。赤身の魚は身の味が濃いので、香りが強いこいくち醤油とかつお出汁の方が合います。この違いは麺つゆの違いにも見られます。関西のうどんのつゆはうすくち醤油を使うので色が薄いですが、関東ではこいくち醤油を使うのでつゆの色も濃くなります。でも、どちらもおいしいので両方試してみるといいでしょう。

■刺身に使う魚の傾向　　　　　　　　■うどんや蕎麦のつゆ

 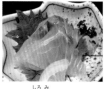   

赤身（関東）　　白身（関西）　　こいくち醤油（関東）　　うすくち醤油（関西）

この他にも、関東と関西の違いには色々おもしろいものがあります。その代表的なものを以下にいくつか挙げますから、是非自分の目でも確かめてみて下さい。

	関 東	関 西
●いなり寿司：関西は三角形だが、関東はたわら型をしている。		
●にぎりめし：関東では「おにぎり」と呼び、三角形で焼き海苔を使う。関西では「おむすび」と呼び、たわら型で味付け海苔を使う。		
●お雑煮(正月料理)：関東では醤油仕立てで、餅は四角いところが多い。関西では味噌仕立てで、餅は丸い。		
●ねぎ：関東では白い部分が多い白ねぎ(長ねぎ)がよく使われる。関西では青い部分が多い青ねぎが一般的。		

●内容質問

1 関東と関西の出汁の違いを説明して下さい。

2 関東と関西の醤油の違いを説明して下さい。

3 関東と関西の刺身の違いは何ですか。

4 関東と関西で、形や味が違う料理を三つあげて下さい。

●発展問題

1 本文で紹介した食べ物以外でも、関東と関西の違いがあります。調べてみましょう。

2 食文化以外で、関東と関西の地域差にはどのようなものがあるか、話し合ってみましょう。

3 皆さんの国の中には、どのような文化圏の違いがありますか。

4 文化圏の違いが食文化にも現れていますか。

「くだらない」の意味と食べ物

　関西（京都と大阪）のことを「上方」と呼びます。これは元々日本の文化の中心は関西で「上」、江戸は田舎だったので「下」と考えていたからです。江戸時代には京都・大阪から江戸に来ることを「下る」と言いました。同様に、大阪から来た物を「下り物」と呼び、その中には「下り酒」「下り醤油」「下り米」などがありました。どれも「江戸にはない高級なもの」という意味で使われていました。そこで、質がよくないもの、価値がないものは「江戸には下らない」という意味で、「くだらない」ということばが使われるようになりました。今では「くだらない」は「程度がひくい、ばからしい」などの意味で使われています。

レシピ

月見蕎麦（関東のつゆ）

関東は蕎麦文化、関西はうどん文化だといわれます。関東蕎麦のつゆは色が濃く、醤油の風味が強いのが特徴。一方、関西のうどんのつゆは色が薄く、うま味と塩気のきいた出汁のおいしさで食べます。

●材料（1人分）

蕎麦（乾麺）.................................1人分

卵 1個

水 400ml

A 和風顆粒だし.................... 小さじ 1/2

こいくち醤油 .... 大さじ 2

みりん......................... 大さじ 1+1/2

青ねぎ ....少々

●作り方

1 小鍋に水とAを入れて沸騰させ、かけつゆを作る。

2 鍋にたっぷりの湯を沸かし、仕上がりに合わせて乾麺をゆではじめる。ゆで時間は袋の記載に従う（標準は 7~8 分程度）。

3 蓋つきの小フライパンに 1 のかけつゆ 150ml 程度をとり、火にかける。卵を割り入れ、蓋をして 30 秒から 1 分程中火で煮立てて火を止める。余熱で好みのかたさまで火を通す。

4 青ねぎを小口切りにする。

5 ゆで上がった麺をザルにあげて湯をきり、器に入れる。1 を温め、熱々のかけつゆを注ぐ。3 の卵とねぎをのせる。

料理のことば 割り入れる, 余熱, 小口切り, 湯をきる, ➡ p.138

TIPS

・蕎麦はそのままにしておくと柔らかくなるので（「蕎麦がのびる」と言う）、できたらすぐ食べましょう。

・七味唐辛子を少しかけてもおいしいです。

・市販の麺つゆを使う場合は「温かいめん（かけつゆ）」の表示に従って水で薄めます。

第3章　出汁とうま味

　出汁は「和食の命」と言われるほど日本料理にとって大切なものです。おいしい料理を作るにはおいしい出汁が欠かせません。出汁の語源は「煮出し汁」で、辞書には「かつお節や昆布などを煮出して作る、うまみのある汁」とあります（「デジタル大辞泉」2021.4.10閲覧）。

日本料理の出汁に使われる食材の代表的なものは昆布、かつお節、煮干し、干しシイタケなどです。出汁は料理にうま味成分を足し、風味を増し、料理全体の味を引き立たせる役をします。

　「うま味」は現在は化学的に人間の舌が感じられる五つ目の味と認識されています。しかし、欧米がこれを認めたのは比較的最近のことです。従来、欧米では味覚の基本は四つ（甘味、酸味、塩味、苦味）とされていました^{（＊）}。1908年に池田菊苗という化学者が昆布に含まれるグルタミン酸の研究を通して発見した五つ目の味として「うま味」が加えられ、1980年代後半に世界的に知られるようになりました。旨い味、おいしい味という意味の「旨み、旨味」はdelicious tasteと英訳できますが、五つ目の味である「うま味」はumamiと表記されます。

　西洋料理のスープストックや中国料理の湯（タン）も広い意味で「出汁」と言えます。材料は肉、魚、野菜が中心で、それらを長時間煮込んで味を作り出します。うま味成分も多く出ているのですが、その他の味を感じさせる成分が多く出ているので複雑な味になり、うま味成分を単体で味わうのは難しいかもしれません。一方、日本料理では、かつお節や昆布など出汁をとるための食品を使うことと、出汁をとるためにかかる時間が短いことが特徴と言えます。かつお節や昆布からはうま味成分が主に出て他の成分はあまり出ないため、出汁を飲むと「うま味」をしっかり感じることができます。出汁に少し塩を入

昆布・干しシイタケ
かつお節・煮干し

れて飲んでみると、うま味を強く感じます。人が感じるうま味成分はグルタミン酸、イノシン酸、グアニル酸の三つに大きく分けられます。グルタミン酸は昆布に多く含まれ、イノシン酸はかつお節や煮干し、グアニル酸は干しシイタケに多く含まれています。合わせ出汁によって異なるうま味成分を組み合わせることで、うま味を強く感じるようになります。

昆布：

　昆布は北海道や東北地方の冷たい海で採れる海藻の一種です。長さは3メートルぐらいになるものもあります。昆布は天日干しして、乾燥した形で市販されています。昆布は干して保存しておくと、渋味が少なくなり甘味に似たおいしい味わいがでてきます。これが昆布のうま味成分であるグルタミン酸です。現在日本の昆布の90％以上は北海道で生産されています。江戸時代には北海道と大阪を北陸周りで繋いでいた北前船（西廻り航路）に乗って、昆布が大量に西日本にもたらされ昆布出汁の文化が形成されます。また、北前船は薩摩藩（現在の鹿児島県）を通じて、中国に昆布を輸出したので、その中継地だった琉球王国（現在の沖縄県）でも昆布が使われるようになりました（→「めしあがれウェブ」地図参照）。現在でも沖縄には昆布を使った郷土料理がたくさんあります。

海中

天日干し

乾燥昆布

かつお節：

　かつお節はカツオの身を煮てから燻し、乾燥させたものを指します。さらに特殊なカビをつけて発酵させた本枯れ節というかつお節もあります。モルディブなどカツオが獲れる海域では似たような加工品がありますが、本枯れ節は日本だけのもので、水分を15％程度

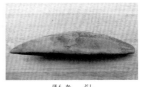
本枯れ節

20

しか含まず、一見すると木片のようです。とても固く、世界で一番固い食べ物と言われています。実は、「かつお」という名前も「堅魚（かたうお）」から来たと言われていて、日本人は古くから干して保存食にしていたようです。

　現在のようなかつお節は紀州（現在の和歌山県）で15世紀に初めて作られ、江戸時代には土佐（高知県）、薩摩（鹿児島県）、焼津（静岡県）などでも質のいいかつお節が作られるようになりました。

　かつお節を作る工場では、まずカツオの身を三枚におろし、それを湯でゆっくり煮ます。そのあと、燻して乾燥させます。これを繰り返すことで、身から水分が抜けて固くなります。その次に、さらに水分を取るためにカビ付けという作業をおこなって、また干します。このように数ヶ月以上かけてできたかつお節はとても固くなりますが、その中にはうま味成分のイノシン酸がたくさん詰まっています。

　かつお節から出汁をとるときは、かつお節を薄く削って削り節を作らなければなりません。昔は、どの家でもその日に使う分だけ毎日かつお節を削っていました。最近は、あらかじめ削ってある削り節パックをスーパーで買うことができるようになったので、削る必要がなくなりました。

※　胡椒や唐辛子、わさびなどから感じるいわゆる「辛味」は物理的な刺激であり、舌が感じる味覚（化学的な刺激）の一つには入っていません。

●内容質問

1 「和食の命」の意味は何ですか。

2 「出汁」の役目は何ですか。

3 「うま味」を説明して下さい。

4 「かつお節」はどうやって作られますか。

●発展問題

1 皆さんの国では、どんな出汁（あるいはスープストック）がありますか。

2 日本以外で昆布を食材にしている国があるか調べて下さい。

3 菜食主義者の人はどの出汁を使えばいいと思いますか。

4 皆さんの国で使う食材で、うま味成分（グルタミン酸、イノシン酸、グアニル酸）が豊富

　な食材を探してレポートして下さい。

食感のことば

　日本語は食感を表すことばが豊富です。代表的なものを紹介しますが、他に
もたくさんあります。

> カラッと　サクサク　ジューシー　ふわふわ　シャキシャキ　パサパサ
> カリカリ　もちもち　口あたりがいい・なめらか

・この唐揚げ、**カラッと**揚がっていて、衣が**サクサク**していてとてもおいしい。

　中はとても**ジューシー**。

・この親子丼、卵が**ふわふわ**です。

・野菜が新鮮で**シャキシャキ**しています。

・この煮魚、身がかたくて**パサパサ**してる。（マイナスイメージの言葉です）

・このパン、外は**カリカリ**で中は**もちもち**していておいしい。

・クリームを入れると、**口あたりがよく**（**なめらかに**）なります。

だし巻き卵

卵焼きは、お弁当に入れるおかずの定番で子どもが大好きなメニューです。そば屋でお酒のつまみ（酒肴）に頼む人もいます。

●材料

卵	....	3個
水	....	大さじ 4（60ml）
和風顆粒だし	....	小さじ 1/4
A 醤油	....	小さじ 1/4
みりん	....	小さじ 1
塩	....	ひとつまみ
油	....	小さじ 1
大根おろし	....	適宜
醤油	....	適宜

●作り方

1 ボウルに卵を入れて白身を切るようによく混ぜる。

2 水に顆粒だしを溶き、1 に加える。A の調味料も加えて混ぜる。

3 卵焼き器を中弱火にかけ、油を入れる。小さく切ったキッチンペーパーで油を薄くのばし、余分な油を拭き取る。

4 2 の卵液の 1/5 ～ 1/6 を流し込み、向こう側から手前に巻く。

5 巻いた卵を向こう側に動かし、手前に油をしく。同様に卵液がなくなるまで 4 を繰り返す。

6 まな板に取り出し、食べやすい大きさに切って皿に盛る。

7 大根おろしを添えて、醤油をかける。

料理のことば 溶く，塩ひとつまみ ➡ p.138

TIPS

- 卵焼き器は四角いフライパンです。なければ、丸いフライパンでもできますが、厚さが均一になりません。

- 砂糖（大さじ 2）を入れると甘い卵焼き（厚焼き卵）になります。甘さは好みで調整してください。

　和食の中で不動の人気を誇る「寿司／鮨」は国境
を越えて世界中の色々な所でおいしい料理として認
識されるようになりました。今では、SUSHIでその
まま通じるようになりました。しかし、一言に寿司
といっても、右の写真のようなものだけでなく、日
本各地に実に色々な種類のものがあります。

握り寿司

　「すし」は元々「酸っぱいご飯」という意味の「すし飯」を語源とする説が一番
妥当なようです。寿司のルーツは諸説ありますが、紀元前3世紀頃、東南アジア
の農耕民が魚を長期に食べられるように保存食として作り出したというのが一般
的です。魚に塩と米飯を足して、数ヶ月間つけ込んで、乳酸発酵させました。出
来上がった時には米は溶けてしまってドロドロになっているので、洗い流して魚
の肉だけを食べました。

　それが中国を経て、日本に伝わりました。9世紀頃に「なれずし」と呼ばれる
魚肉の保存食としてのすし(鮓)が作られていた記録があり、それが日本の寿司の
始まりだと言えます。魚、塩、ご飯を一緒に数ヶ月
間つけ込んで、食べる時はご飯を洗って魚だけを食
べました。現在でも滋賀県にある「ふなずし」は、
「なれずし」としての形を継承しています。14世紀に
なると、米も一緒に食べられるようにした「なまな
れ」「飯ずし」などと呼ばれる寿司が登場しました。
今でも日本各地に郷土料理として残っています。

ふなずし

　室町時代には「箱寿司」「押し寿司」と呼ばれるタ
イプの寿司が関西で作られるようになります。塩漬
けにした魚をご飯と一緒に箱に入れて押したり、棒
状に形を整えて漬けました。現在の「大阪寿司」と

押し寿司

呼ばれるものや、「さば寿司」などの原型にあたるものです。

　江戸時代に入ると「酢」の製造方法が確立され、大量生産が可能になります。そして、江戸時代中期(17世紀)には、乳酸発酵をさせて酸っぱくする代わりに、酢を混ぜたご飯を使った「早寿司」と呼ばれる寿司が生まれました。「笹巻けぬきすし」というこのような寿司を初めて作ったと言われている店が現在でも東京で営業しています。

笹東都名所 高輪二十六夜待遊興之図
歌川広重　太田美術館所蔵

　そして、いよいよ19世紀の始めに、華屋与兵衛という江戸の寿司職人によって「握り寿司」が発明されました(※1)。これが現在一般的に「江戸前寿司」と言われているスタイルです(※2)。そして、これが世界的にSUSHIとして認識されている料理の原型です。当時は天ぷらなど色々な種類の食べ物の屋台があり、握り寿司も屋台で出されていました。ちょうど現在のキッチンカーみたいな感じです。冷蔵庫のような保存設備のないその頃の寿司は、ご飯に酢を混ぜて「すし飯」を作り、魚は悪くならないように火を通したり(煮ハマグリ、煮アナゴなど)、酢漬けにしたり(コハダ)、醤油漬け(マグロの赤身)にしたりしていました。醤油漬けにしたものを「づけ」とよび、現在でもマグロの寿司をづけで出すお店があります。

　明治時代になると製氷技術が発達し、魚を冷蔵しておくことが可能になります。

撮影協力：鮨 一新（浅草）

この頃寿司は、まだ基本的に関東のものでした。それが現在のように全国的に知られるようになった理由の一つに1923年の関東大震災があります。この災害で東京は甚大な被害を受け、東京の寿司屋で働いていた地方出身の職人達が故郷に帰るなどして全国に散らばりました。そして、その結果、江戸前寿司が全国に広がりました。

　1950年代頃から寿司屋には「高い」というイメージが定着していきましたが、1960年代に大阪で店内にベルトコンベアーがあり、その上に乗って回ってくる寿

司を客が自分で取って食べるという「回転寿司」が出現しま
した。取ったお皿の枚数で値段を計算するので、会計が明朗
であることと値段が安かったので、人気が出ました。現在は
回転寿司店も多様化し、ラーメンやデザートなど寿司以外の
メニューの数も増えました。

回転寿司

　1980年代になると寿司は日本だけに留まらず、海外でも注目されSUSHIとして
紹介され、人気がでました。日本人が西洋料理を自分達の舌に合った物に変えて
いったように、外国でも独自のSUSHIが展開されています。その中の代表的なも
のの一つが「カリフォルニアロール」でしょう。海苔が内側にくるように巻いた
寿司は、アメリカ人が外側に海苔があるのをあまり好まなかったのが理由だそう
です。今ではこのような巻き方は「裏巻き」と呼ばれています。この他にも、色々
な材料を入れて巻いたSUSHIが海外では人気があるようです。皆さんの国にはど
んなSUSHIがありますか。

カリフォルニアロール

※1　握り寿司の発明者には諸説ありますが、本書では華屋与兵衛とする説を採用しました。
※2　元々「江戸前」というのは「江戸の前にある海」つまり東京湾です。ですから東京湾でとれた
　　　材料を使った寿司を「江戸前の寿司」と言っていましたが、現在は握り寿司のスタイルそのもの
　　　を指すようになりました。

●内容質問

1 「すし」という言葉の語源は何ですか。

2 9世紀頃の寿司はどんな食べ物でしたか。

3 「江戸前寿司」はどんな寿司ですか。そして、どのようにして全国に広がりましたか。

4 「回転寿司」はいつ頃できましたか。どんな寿司ですか。

●発展問題

1 皆さんの国にはどんな寿司がありますか。日本の寿司とは何が違いますか。

2 寿司は元々保存食でしたが、皆さんの国にはどのような保存食がありますか。

3 特定の地域で食べられている寿司や古い形の寿司について調べてレポートして下さい。

4 海外の寿司屋の名前にはおもしろいものがたくさんあります。皆さんの国にある寿司屋の
  名前を調べてレポートして下さい。

column
食の
ひとくち
メモ
「さかな」の語源

　現在「さかな」ということばは「魚」の漢字を使って、英語の fish の意味で
使われていますが、室町時代までは意味も漢字も違っていました。「さかな」は
元々「お酒を飲む時に一緒に食べる物」のことで、漢字は「酒菜」でした。で
すから、漬物や味噌なども「酒菜」でした。江戸時代に魚肉が「酒菜」として
よく使われるようになったため、魚肉のことを「さかな」というようになり、
漢字も「魚」が使われるようになりました。

　魚を指す元々の日本語は「うお」です。現在でも、トビウオ、タチウオなど
特定の魚の名前に残っています。また、昔からある魚屋の名前にも「魚政」「魚
波」など「うお」が入っていることがあります。「魚市場」も「うおいちば」と
読みます。

　お酒を飲む時に食べるもの（「つまみ」とも言う）は、現在でも「さかな」と
いいますが、漢字は「肴」を使います。

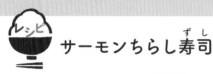

サーモンちらし寿司

ちらし寿司は、ひな祭りなどの行事食（ぎょうじしょく）として家庭でもよく作られます。寿司飯（すしめし）の作り方がわかれば、家庭でもいろいろな具材をのせてちらし寿司のバリエーションを楽しめます。

材料（2人分）

米 .... 1合（150g）
（出来上がり約350gの寿司飯（すしめし））

＜寿司酢（すしず）＞
米酢（こめず）(or 穀物酢（こくもつず）) .... 大さじ1+1/2
砂糖 大さじ1
塩 小さじ1/4

＜錦糸卵（きんしたまご）＞
卵 1個
砂糖 小さじ1
塩 .... ひとつまみ
油 .... 少々
スモークサーモン 30g
カニかまぼこ 50g
さやえんどう .... 2~3枚
海苔（のり） .... 適量

作り方

1 米をかために炊く（たく）（炊飯器（すいはんき）のメモリよりほんの少しだけ水を少なくする）。

2 酢に砂糖と塩を溶かして寿司酢を作る。

3 炊きたての熱いご飯に寿司酢をかけて均一（きんいつ）に混ぜ寿司飯（すしめし）を作り、冷ましておく。

4 卵に砂糖と塩を加えてよくかき混ぜ、油をしいたフライパンに薄く（うすく）広げて焼く。冷めたら細く切り錦糸卵（きんしたまご）を作る。

5 湯を沸かし（わかし）少量の塩（分量外（ぶんりょうがい））を入れて、さやえんどうを1分ほどゆでる。冷水にとり、色止め（いろどめ）をする。

6 皿に寿司飯をよそい、その上に細く切った（またはちぎった）海苔と錦糸卵をのせ、スモークサーモン、カニかまぼこ、さやえんどうをのせる。

料理のことば 塩ひとつまみ, かため, 分量外, 色止め, ちぎる ➡ p.138

🍳 TIPS ・ のせる具材として錦糸卵は定番ですが、その他は自由に組み合わせてください。（ぐざい）

第5章 洋食のはじまり

海外で「Kobe beef」という言葉は高級ステーキを指す言葉として通用しますし、オーストラリアで育てられている「wagyu」という言葉も聞かれるようになりました。しかし、日本人が牛肉を食べ始めたのはそんなに昔のことではありません。

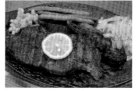

ステーキ

19世紀後半、明治維新で鎖国時代が終わった日本には「文明開化」の号令の下に、西洋文化が急速に入り込んできました。日本政府は日本人の体格が西洋人に比べて大きく劣ることに危機感を感じ、肉や卵、牛乳・乳製品を食べることを奨励します。日本では天皇が7世紀に発令した肉食禁止令によって、獣の肉を食べることが禁じられていました。そのため、日本人はおよそ1,200年間、牛、豚、鶏などの家畜を育てて肉を食べるということをしてきませんでした。ですから、いくら政府が奨励しても、食べ慣れていない日本人にとっては難しいことで、「肉を食べると体が汚れる」と考えていた人もたくさんいたそうです。そして、このような状況のなかで牛鍋という料理ができました。それが今日の「すき焼き」の始まりです。

すき焼き

20世紀にはいると西洋料理を日本人の食の好みに合わせてアレンジした料理がたくさん作り出され、「日本化した西洋料理」という意味で「洋食」と呼ばれるようになりました。本章ではその典型として現在でも人気がある「とんかつ」と「カレーライス」を例にとって見ていきましょう。

とんかつ:

とんかつは小麦粉、溶き卵、パン粉から作った衣で豚肉を包んで、たくさんの油で揚げた料理です。豚のロース肉とヒレ肉を使うのが一般的です。ロース肉は脂身が多く、ヒレ肉は脂身がない柔らかい肉です。

「とんかつ」の「かつ」はフランス語のcoteletteを日本語で発音した「カツレツ」から来ています。「とん」は「豚」の音読みなので、とんかつはフランス語と日本語を混ぜた造語です。明治初期には西洋料理の店では「ポークカツレツ」という言葉が使われていて、食べる時もナイフとフォークを使っていました。

とんかつ

　ポークカツレツは比較的薄い肉を少量の油で調理していました。しかし、1930年頃たっぷりの油の中でステーキのように厚く切った肉を揚げることで、ボリュームがあって、しかも柔らかいとんかつが出来上がりました。そして、それを箸で食べやすいようにあらかじめ切って出しました。こうしてとんかつをキャベツのせん切り、味噌汁、漬け物、茶碗飯と一緒に食べる形が出来上がり、今ではとんかつは和食のように扱われるようになりました。また、とんかつによく合うソースも作り出され、とんかつソースとしてどこのスーパーでも売られています。

カレーライス：

　もう一つの代表的な洋食はカレーライスです。カレーライスは日本人にとって、家庭の料理としても外食の料理としても最も人気がある食べ物の一つです。全日本カレー工業協同組合の統計によると、日本人は一年間に平均60回から70回ぐらいカレーを食べて

カレーライス

る計算になるという結果があります。カレーは日本人の食生活にとって欠かせない料理です。

　カレーの発祥地インドには香辛料をたくさん使った料理やスープがあります。しかし、その中にいわゆる日本のカレーにあたる食べ物はありません。しかも、インドの言葉には「カレー」という言葉すらありません。カレー（curry）の語源は、イギリス植民地時代にイギリス人が聞いたタミール語の「カリ(kari)」（スープをかけたご飯）かヒンズー語の「ターカリ(turcarri)」（香り高いもの）のどちらかのようです。

　カレーは17世紀にイギリスに渡り、ヨーロッパ風にアレンジされていきました。

しかし、料理ごとにたくさんの香辛料を調合することに慣れていなかったので、Crosse & Blackwellという会社があらかじめ調合した香辛料をカレー粉として18世紀後半に商品化しました。

　明治時代に、カレー粉がイギリスによって日本にもたらされ、米飯と結びついて「ライスカレー」になりました。この料理はカレー粉に小麦粉を足してとろみをつけ、西洋料理店で高級料理として出されていました。

　始めは輸入に頼っていたカレー粉も、1920年代に初めての国産カレーパウダーが作ら

カレーパウダー　　　　　カレールー

れ、その後、肉や野菜を煮込んだ後に入れるだけで簡単にカレーが作れるカレールウが開発されました。

　また、蕎麦屋が和洋折衷料理としてカレー南蛮やカレーうどんなどのメニューを作ったり、パン屋がカレーをパンの中に入れて、油で揚げたカレーパンなど、日本独自のカレー料理が作り出されています。1950年代には次々に様々な味(辛さなど)のカレールウが発売され、また、1960年代終わりには世界で初めてのレトルト食品としてレトルトカレーが発売され、カレーライスは一般家庭に急速に浸透していきました。

カレーうどん　　　　　　カレーパン

●内容質問

1 「文明開化」を説明して下さい。

2 日本人はどのぐらいの間、牛肉を食べていませんでしたか。

3 「ポークカツレツ」と「とんかつ」の違いは何ですか。

4 カレーはどのようにして日本に伝えられましたか。

●発展問題

1 文明開化で外国から日本に入ってきたものについて調べてレポートして下さい。

2 とんかつの他に、外国から入ってきて日本の料理としてアレンジされたものにはどんなものがありますか。

3 皆さんの国にもカレーはありますか。それはどこから来たか調べてレポートして下さい。

4 皆さんの国では、外国から入ってきて自分の国の料理としてアレンジされたものがありますか。

パン粉と生パン粉

　とんかつやコロッケなどのいわゆる揚げ物に欠かせないパン粉は元々ヨーロッパのものでした。乾かしたパンを細かく砕いて、衣に使ったり、チーズの代わりにグラタンの上に振りかけたりします。英語では breadcrums と言います。日本のとんかつ専門店では、食パンを乾かさずに砕いた「生パン粉」を使っているところもあります。生パン粉はヨーロッパのパン粉よりも粒が大きくて、水分を多く含んでいます。これで揚げ物を作るとサクッとした食感を出すことができます。日本のスーパーでは生パン粉とパン粉の両方が売られています。一度試してみて下さい。このようなパン粉は海外にはなかったのですが、最近は PANKO という商品名で売られるようになりました。

とんかつ

とんかつにせん切りキャベツは定番のつけあわせで、とんかつ屋ではキャベツのおかわりが自由のところもあります。とんかつはお弁当のおかずに入れたり、醤油味の出汁で卵と一緒に煮てかつ丼にアレンジもできます。

●材料（2人分）

厚切り豚肉（ロース、ヒレなど）……2枚	
小麦粉…………………大さじ 3~4（約40g）	
卵 ………………………………………1個	
パン粉（乾燥または生）…………1カップ	
揚げ油 …………………………………適量	
キャベツ ……………………………2枚程度	
レモン、トマト、パセリ ………………適量	
練りがらし ……………………………適量	
とんかつソース ………………………適量	

●作り方

1　豚肉のスジに包丁で切れ目を入れる。

2　ボウルに卵を入れて溶く。豚肉に小麦粉、溶き卵、パン粉の順にまぶしてつける。

3　フライパンに揚げ油を 3~5cm 程度入れ、160~170℃位に温める。2 の豚肉を入れ、2分くらい揚げたらひっくり返し、さらに 2分くらい揚げたら一旦取り出す。

4　次に油の温度を 180℃に上げて、豚肉をフライパンにもどし、こんがりきつね色になるまで 1~2分かけてもう一度揚げる。

5　キャベツはせん切りにする。つけあわせにキャベツ、レモン、トマト、パセリ、練りがらし、とんかつソースを添える。

料理のことば 切れ目を入れる，溶く，まぶす，こんがりきつね色，せん切り，つけあわせ ➡ p.138

TIPS
　・肉の厚さに応じて揚げる時間を調整してください。厚い場合には片面 3~4分ずつ揚げます。

　・肉の部位の名称は国によって違います。日本では「ロース、ヒレ」と呼びます。

第6章　米

米は小麦、トウモロコシと並んで、世界の三大穀物の一つです。世界の米の約9割はアジアで生産され、消費されています。生産量は中国が一位で、二位はインドです。

米はイネという植物の収穫物で、インディカ種とジャポニカ種に大別されます。インディカ種の米は粒が細長く（長粒種）、炊いたときに粘り気がなくパラパラになるので、他の具材と一緒に混ぜて食べる料理に使います。東南アジアやインド料理によく使われます。これに対して、ジャポニカ種の米は粒が短く（短粒種）、飯には粘り気を感じます。日本では「白ご飯」と呼んで、白米を炊いた白飯を他の料理と一緒に口に入れて口中調味（味の変化を口の中で楽しむ食べ方）して食べる習慣があります。

米の種類をうるち米ともち米に分ける分類もあります。インディカ種にもジャポニカ種にもそれぞれうるち米ともち米があります。日本ではジャポニカ種のうるち米のイネを、水をはった水田で栽培します。水田での稲作は連作障害が起こりづらいので、日本では毎年同じ水田でイネを繰り返し育てる風景が見られます。うるち米の品種には「コシヒカリ」、「あきたこまち」、「ひとめぼれ」などの銘柄があります。この中で、一番人気があるのは「コシヒカリ」という品種で、日本で栽培されているイネの約三分の一に当たります。もち米は餅を作るためのイネです。また、日本酒を作るための酒造米と呼ばれる違った種類のイネも栽培されています。

日本の米は炊くとつやが出て、食感がふっくらと柔らかく粘りがあり、よく噛むと甘味が増します。また、冷めても味が変わらないので、おにぎり、寿司、弁当などにしてもおいしく食べられます。米は日本人にとって、文字どおり主食で、

米を炊いたご飯と一緒に食べる料理を「おかず」と呼びます。日本人は白いご飯と相性の良いおかずに出会うと、「これはご飯がすすみますね。」と言って褒めたりします。和食には「一汁三菜」という言葉がありますが、これはご飯を中心にして、汁が一つとおかずが

一汁三菜

三つという意味で、米をいかに食べるかという考えを反映していると言えます。

　イネは紀元前9～10世紀にアジア大陸から日本に入ってきたと言われています。梅雨時に雨がたくさん降り、夏に気温が高く日照量が多くなるという日本の気候に合い、全国で栽培されるようになりました。弥生時代の水田による栽培の遺跡が日本各地に残っています。また、日本の神話には神の一人が地上に降りてくる時に高天原(神が住む世界)からイネを持ってきたという逸話があります。つまり、日本には米は神がもたらした特別な物であるという考え方が古くからあったのです。現在でも様々な儀式の中で、お神酒(酒)や塩と共に、米が神への感謝を表す供物として使われています。神社で神に供える食べ物を「神饌」と呼びますが、米、稲穂、ご飯、餅、酒など米から作られるものをよくお供えします。また、仏壇がある家では、先祖が食べるためのものという意味で、ご飯を盛った小さな器(仏飯器)を飾る習慣があります。

仏壇のお供え

　このように米は古くから食物として重要で、さらに長期保存が可能だったため、富の象徴となりました。そして、米をたくさん持っている者が裕福であるという認識が広がっていき、経済的に重要な位置を占めるようになりました。中世には米が租税として使われるようになりました。江戸時代でも農民は税として米(年貢米)を納め、武士への給料は米で支給され、「石」や「俵」といった米の量を計る単位で表されていました。しかし、実際に稲作に携わっている農民は必ずしも米だけのご飯を食べていたわけではありません。通常は米に粟やひえなどの雑穀を混ぜて食べていました。

　稲作は日本の政府により、他の作物に比べ手厚く保護されています。日本の食料自給率は約40%ですが、主食用の米の自給率は100％ (2018年農林水産省試算)で、国内

生産だけで消費をまかなえる唯一の作物です。それでも、最近は食の多様化のせいで、日本人の米離れが問題視されています。その改善策として学校給食などを通して米の消費量を増やそうという努力がなされています。

●内容質問

1　「イネ」「米」「ご飯」の違いは何ですか。

2　イネにはどんな種類がありますか。それぞれどんな特徴がありますか。

3　日本人はいつ頃から米を食べていますか。米はどこから来ましたか。

4　米は炊いてご飯として食べる以外にも色々な使われ方をします。どんなものがありますか。

●発展問題

1　日本のお金のデザインにもイネが使われているものがあります。どのお金か調べてみましょう。

2　皆さんの国では「米」はどんな役割りをはたしていますか。「米」を何かのシンボルとして使うことがありますか。

3　米を使った料理でどんなものが好きですか。

4　皆さんの国で、シンボルや儀式に使われたりする特別な意味を持った食べ物について調べてレポートしてください。

column
食の
ひとくち
メモ

「落とし蓋」ってどんな蓋？

　「落とし蓋」とは鍋より直径が少し小さい蓋で、鍋の中に入れて（つまり、「落として」）、材料の上に直接のせて使います。少ない煮汁で煮物を作る時に材料をかき混ぜなくても煮汁を全体にゆき渡らせ、材料の温度を高く保ち、材料が崩れないように煮ることができます。木製のものが多いですが、金属製のものや合成樹脂でできたものもあります。また、落とし蓋がない時にはアルミホイルやオーブンペーパーで簡単に作ることもできます。煮魚を作ったりする時にも重宝します。

レシピ

炊き込みご飯（鶏五目めし）

ご飯ものの「おふくろの味」といえば炊き込みご飯が代表選手。具材の組み合わせと味付けで、家庭の味が出ます。鶏肉と野菜類を入れて醤油味の五目ご飯、グリンピースなどの豆を入れて塩味の豆ご飯とバリエーションと多様です。

材料（4人分）

米 ....2合（300g）
＜具材＞
　鶏もも肉 120g
　人参 40g
　ごぼう 30g
　たけのこ水煮 30g
　こんにゃく 40g
　油揚げ 20g
　しめじ 20g
　えのきだけ 20g
水 390ml

A 酒 大さじ2
　塩 小さじ1/2
　醤油 大さじ1
青ねぎ ....少々

作り方

1 米をといで水に30分つけた後、ザルにあげて水を切る。

2 ごぼうはささがきにして水にさらす。こんにゃくは短冊切りにして、2-3分ゆでてアクを抜く。油揚げは熱湯をかけて油ぬきをしたあと、短冊切りにする。

3 人参はいちょう切りに、たけのこ水煮は細切りにする。しめじとえのきだけは石づきを取る。鶏肉を1cm角に切る。

4 厚手の鍋に1の米を入れ、水とAを加え、2、3の具材をのせる。

5 蓋をして中弱火にかけて7~8分かけて沸騰させる。加熱途中は蓋は開けない。蓋の間から水蒸気が出て沸騰したらすぐに弱火にする。12~15分弱火で加熱し、水分がなくなり水蒸気が出なくなったら火を止め、そのまま蓋を開けずに10分間蒸らす。12分より前でも焦げたにおいがしてきたらすぐに火を止め、10分蒸らす。

6 蓋を開けて全体をかき混ぜる。お茶碗によそい、仕上げに刻んだ青ねぎをのせる。

料理のことば ささがき，短冊切り，油ぬき，いちょう切り，○cm角 ➡ p.138

TIPS
・炊き込みご飯の具材と米の割合は、重量比で1：1～1：2が基準です。米100gに対して、豆ごはんなら50gの豆を、鶏五目めしのように具材を組み合わせて入れる場合は計100gの具材を入れます。

・ごぼうはピーラーでささがきにしてもよい。

　箸は日本を含め、主に東アジア諸国で使われている
食具で、一番古い記録は紀元前14世紀の中国にあるそ
うです。日本には6世紀頃仏教とともに大陸から伝わっ
たとされています。中国の有名な歴史書「三国志」の中

の魏志倭人伝（当時の中国が日本について書いた記録）には弥生時代の日本人は食
べ物を手で食べていたという記述があります。現在、世界の人口の約30％は箸を、
約30％がナイフとフォークを、残りの約40％が手を使って食べる文化圏となって
います。

　箸を使う国々の間でも、それぞれの国の食文化の変化
に伴い、箸の形状や使い方が少しずつ違います。例えば、
中国の箸は日本のものよりも長く、先が尖っていません。
そして、レンゲというスプーンのような食具と一緒に使
います。これは中国料理は大皿で出され、それを各自が
取り分けて食べるという習慣があったことが理由のよう
です。韓国では金属製の細い箸が使われるようになり、

韓国の金属製食器

箸とさじ（スプーン）の両方を使って食べます。レンゲやさじなど汁物をすくう食具
を使う中国や韓国では、器を持ち上げて口をつけて汁を飲むのはマナー違反です。

　これに対して、日本ではさじが食具として定着しなかったので、箸だけを使う
ようになりました。その結果、味噌汁などの汁物はお椀を手に持って、直接口をつ
けて汁を飲むようになりました。汁が熱い時は、冷ますために息を吹きかけたり、
空気を吸いながら飲む、つまり「すする」という食べ方をするようになりました。
その結果、すする時に出てしまう音に対しても寛容に
なったと考えられます。また、お椀はもともと木で作ら
れていたのであまり熱くならず持ち上げやすかったので
しょう。さらに、日本では昔から焼いた魚をそのまま食

卓に出していたので、魚の身をほぐして、小さい骨を取り除くために箸の先が細く尖っていたほうが便利でした。また、箸は小さいものをはさんだり、柔らかい物を切ったりするのに使います。ただし、箸を突き刺して食べるのは行儀が悪いとされているので、滑りやすい物や柔らかい物を食べるのには練習が必要です。

　箸には用途によっていくつか種類がありますが、最も一般的なのは普段食べる時に使う個人用の箸です。日本の家庭では家族一人一人の箸やご飯茶碗が決まっていて、いつも同じ箸と茶碗を使って食べる習慣があります。個人用の箸は、木製、竹製、プラスチック製など材料も様々で、安い物から高価な物まで色々あります。中には、「塗り箸」と呼ばれる伝統的な漆塗りの技術を使った大変きれいな物もあります。可愛いデザインの箸もたくさんありますから、箸の専門店に行って、自分専用の箸を一膳見つけてみるといいでしょう。

　この他にも、料理をする時に使う菜箸、大皿の料理を自分の皿に取るときの取り箸、パーティや弁当などで用意される使い捨ての割り箸など用途に応じて色々な種類の箸が使われています。

　箸の使い方にはいくつかマナーがあります。代表的な例を三つあげます。一つ目は茶碗に入っているご飯に箸を立てて刺すのは「立て箸」と呼ばれ、良くないマナーです。これはお葬式の時に亡くなった人にご飯を捧げる時に箸を立てる習慣があるからです。二つ目は食べ物を自分の箸から他人の箸へ渡すことです。これは「合わせ箸」、または「箸渡し」と呼ばれ、悪いマナーとされています。三つ目は「違い箸」といって、長さや材質の違う2本の箸を組み合わせて使うことも良くないです。仏教では亡くなった人を火葬した後に、箸を使って骨を拾う習慣がありますが、その時に長さの違う箸で、骨を箸から箸に渡すのが正しい方法なのです。死に通じる場面での箸の使い方は「縁起が悪い」と言って悪いマナーとされています。

　箸を置く時に、先がテーブルにつかないようにする「箸おき」という小さなアクセサリーを使うことがあります。日本ではユニークなものから伝統的なものまで、色々な箸おきが売られているので、気に入ったのを集めてみるのもおもしろいでしょう。

●内容質問

1 箸を使う文化圏はどこですか。

2 日本の箸の特徴は何ですか。他の国の箸とどこが違いますか。

3 日本で汁物を食べる時はどうやって食べますか。

4 箸の使い方で悪いマナーにはどのようなものがありますか。

●発展問題

1 「手で食べる」文化圏はどこか調べてみましょう。

2 日本の「塗り箸」で有名な所はどこですか。調べてみましょう。

3 日本以外の国でも個人用の食具を使う文化がありますか。調べてみましょう。

4 蕎麦やうどんを食べるための箸はどのようなデザインになっていると思いますか。調べて
レポートして下さい。

column
食の
ひとくち
メモ

きれいな箸の持ち方

　箸を正しく持つと使いやすいだけでなく、見た目もきれいです。基本は二つあります。まず、下の箸は親指の付け根にはさんで薬指の脇に押し付けて固定します。物を取る時にこの箸は動きません。次に、親指と人差し指と中指の三本の指先で上の箸を動かす練習をします。上の箸の先が下の箸の先にうまく重なるようになれば、米粒のようなとても小さな物でも箸ではさんで取れるようになります。

味噌汁
（みそしる）

味噌汁は米飯には欠かせない定番の汁物です。味噌にも中に入れる実（具材）にもいろいろな種類があります。出汁は煮干し、昆布、かつお節などから取り風味を楽しみます。簡単ですが、奥の深い料理です。

材料（4人分）

煮干し出汁	600ml
水	700ml 程度
煮干し	20g 程度
味噌	大さじ 3 程度
豆腐	1丁（約 300g）
乾燥わかめ	大さじ 3
青ねぎ	1本

作り方

1　煮干しの頭とわた（内臓）を取り除き、水と一緒に鍋に入れる。

2　鍋を火にかけ、沸騰したら弱火にして 10 分ほど煮出す。ザルでこして出汁をとる。

3　乾燥わかめを水でもどす。

4　豆腐を 1.5cm 角程度のさいの目切りにする。青ねぎを小口切りにする。

5　2 でとった煮干し出汁を鍋に入れて火にかけ、沸騰したら豆腐とわかめを入れ、再沸騰したら一旦火を止める。

6　味噌を鍋に入れて溶く。再び火をつけ、味噌汁が熱くなったら青ねぎを加え、お椀にそそぐ。

料理のことば　こす，水でもどす，さいの目切り，小口切り ➡ p.138

TIPS
・よくある味噌汁の実(具材)：豆腐、油揚げ、わかめ、長ねぎ、玉ねぎ、大根、じゃがいも、里いも、しじみ、あさりなど。
・味噌汁はぐらぐら沸騰させない方が出汁と味噌の風味が良くておいしいです。
・顆粒だしを使う場合は、入れすぎないように注意してください。出汁はあくまでも引き立て役です。

第8章　和食の麺（うどん・蕎麦）

　「麺」とは小麦粉や米粉に水と塩などを混ぜて生地を作り、それを細長くした食べ物です。西洋料理で一番有名な麺と言えば、イタリア料理のパスタでしょう。アジアでは中国、ベトナム、カンボジア、タイなどで色々な麺が食べられています。日本の麺と言えば「うどん」と「蕎麦」で、とても人気がある食べ物の一つです。

うどん：

　うどんは小麦の粒を挽いた粉に水と塩を加え、こねてから、長く伸ばしたり切ったりして作ります。塩を入れないものもあります。8世紀頃遣唐使によって中国からもたらされたという説が有力で、その遣唐使の

寄港地でもあった長崎県の五島列島には「五島手延べうどん」という古い形のうどんが今でも残されています。うどんは江戸時代までは貴重な食品で庶民には普及していませんでした。なぜなら、うどんの普及には、小麦を粉にするための石臼が不可欠だったからです。元々、石臼は抹茶を作るためのものが主で、数も少なく、一般の人の手には入りませんでした。その状況が変化したのは15世紀末から16世紀にかけての日本の戦国時代でした。日本各地の領主達が城を盛んに造り、その石垣を造るために石工が全国から集められました。始めは城造りで忙しかった石工達も少しずつ暇になり、余った時間に石臼を作ったそうです。そのおかげで、石臼が手に入りやすくなり、小麦粉が量産できるようになって、江戸時代にはうどんも庶民の食べ物として普及しました。また、米と違って小麦は租税の対象にならなかったので、農民は米を収穫した後の土地で小麦を育て、生活の糧にしていました。

石臼

　こうして江戸時代には、日本中にうどんが広がりました。今でも、日本各地に

は、秋田県の「稲庭うどん」、長野県の「おしぼりうどん」、長崎県の「五島うどん」、三重県の「伊勢うどん」など特徴のある地域のうどんが残っています。

うどんには色々な太さのものと柔らかさのものがあります。うどんのかたさを表現する時には「コシ」という言葉を使います。「このうどんにはコシがある」というのは、歯ごたえがしっかりしているという意味です。どんなうどんでも茹ですぎるとコシはなくなり、柔らかくてふにゃふにゃしたうどんになります。三重県の「伊勢うどん」は長い時間茹でるので、コシがなくとも柔らかいことが特徴のうどんです。

稲庭うどん

五島うどん

伊勢うどん

日本のうどんの中で最も有名なのは香川県の「讃岐うどん」でしょう。コシが強いのが特徴です。香川県は日本で一番小さい県で人口は100万人ほどですが、うどんの一人当たりの消費量は日本一です。県内には900軒ほどのうどん屋があると言われていて、朝ご飯にうどんを食べる人もいて、「うどん県」と呼ばれています。香川県の空の玄関口である高松空港にはうどんの出汁が無料で飲める蛇口があります。

蕎麦（そば）：

蕎麦（そば）の歴史はうどんより長く、約九千年前（縄文時代）の日本ですでにソバの実が栽培されていたようです。イネに比べて、ソバの実は土地が肥沃でなくても育ち、さらに日照りや冷害にも強かったので、救荒作物でした。ただし、米より実が固いソバは江戸時代まで大量に食べられることはありませんでした。

江戸時代の初頭に石臼が普及して、小麦粉と同じように、そば粉がたくさん作れるようになりました。そば粉の料理の始まりは現在のような細い麺のそば

ではなく、団子のようにして煮て食べる「そばがき」という食べ物でした。そして、17世紀初頭にはそば粉を練った生地を伸ばして細く切った「そばきり」という料理ができ、これが現在の蕎麦の麺の元になりました。江戸時代は蕎麦の発達期でした。そば粉だけで作った蕎麦は「十割」とよばれソバの実の風味が強いものです。それに対して小麦粉を二割混ぜた蕎麦は「二八」と呼ばれました。また、ソバの実の中心だけを挽いて作った白く上品な味わいの「更科蕎麦」やソバの実の色が入った薄緑色の「薮蕎麦」などが人気がありました。

　江戸時代後期の江戸には蕎麦屋が3,500軒以上、それに3,000軒以上の蕎麦の屋台があったと言われていますから、江戸の人は蕎麦が大好きだったと想像できます。また、「年越し蕎麦」という大晦日に細くて長い蕎麦を縁起物として食べる習慣も江戸時代にできました。この習慣は今でもたくさんの日本の家庭で行われています。うどんと同様に、日本各地にご当地蕎麦がたくさんあります。その中で、長野県の「戸隠蕎麦」、岩手県の「わんこ蕎麦」、島根県の「出雲蕎麦」が日本の三大蕎麦と言われています。

戸隠蕎麦

わんこ蕎麦

出雲蕎麦

●内容質問
1　和食の麺（うどん、蕎麦）はどうやって作りますか。
2　「石臼」とは何ですか。どうして、石臼がうどんや蕎麦の歴史の中で大切だったのですか。
3　「そばがき」とは何ですか。
4　日本でうどんが有名な県はどこですか。

●発展問題
1　皆さんの国の料理にはどんな麺がありますか。
2　日本の有名なうどんか蕎麦の中から一つ選び、調べてレポートして下さい。
3　皆さんの国では特定の日に食べる特別な食べ物がありますか。
4　日本以外の麺を一つ選んで、材料、作り方、食べ方などを調べてレポートして下さい。

麺の「コシ」ってなに？

　うどんやラーメンの麺について話す時に、よく「コシ」という言葉が出て来ます。「この店の麺はコシがあって、おいしい」という具合に使われます。パスタの「アルデンテ」と似ているようなのですが、実は少し違います。

　アルデンテは茹で具合を表す言葉なのに対して、「コシ」は麺自体の特性を表します。「コシがある」、あるいは、「コシが強い」麺は噛んだ時に歯ごたえがあって、歯が跳ね返るような弾力を感じます。

　また、どんな麺でもゆでたあとすぐに食べないと伸びてしまいます。伸びた麺は歯ごたえがなく、おいしくありません。ですから、麺を食べる時は出来立てを食べるようにしましょう。

手打ちうどん

うどんを自分で作ってみましょう。実は、うどんを粉から手作りするのはそんなに難しくありません。日本人もあまり作らない「手打ちうどん」にぜひ挑戦してみてください。

●材料（2人分）
薄力粉...100g
強力粉...100g
水...95~100ml
塩...10g（小さじ2弱）
打ち粉（強力粉）.........................適量
麺つゆ（2倍希釈）.........................100ml
水...100ml
おろし生姜、青ねぎ.........................適量

●作り方

1 水95mlに塩を入れ完全に溶かす。薄力粉と強力粉を合わせたものに塩水を加え、菜箸で混ぜる。

2 全体がしっとりしてきたら手で混ぜて、一つの生地にまとめる。粉がパサついてまとまらない場合は、水（小さじ1）を加えてぎりぎりまとまるくらいのかたさに調整する。

3 生地を5分ほどこねて均一になったら、ビニール袋に入れて30分~1時間寝かせる。

4 生地を取り出して1分ほどこね、再びビニール袋に入れて15分置く。

5 乾いたまな板に打ち粉（強力粉）を薄くふり、生地を綿棒で厚さ2~3mmに伸ばす。生地の上に打ち粉をたっぷりふり、三つか四つ折りにたたんで、2~3mmの太さに切る。

6 麺の切り口にも打ち粉をふり、麺同士がくっつかないようにバラバラにしておく。

7 鍋にたっぷりの熱湯を沸かし、麺を入れてかき混ぜる。ふきこぼれに注意して7~8分ゆで、冷水に取り出し水洗いして冷やす。麺の水を切り、皿に盛る。

8 麺つゆを水で割り、つけつゆを作る。おろし生姜と青ねぎを添える。

料理のことば　しっとりする，パサつく，寝かせる，ふきこぼれ ➡ p.138

TIPS ・麺は水加減がとても重要です。ベタベタくっつく場合は小麦粉を足してください。

・生地をこねた後に寝かす（休ませる）ことで伸ばしやすくなります。伸ばしにくい時は少し休ませてください。

第9章　弁当と駅弁

　日本の弁当の起源は平安時代の「干し飯」という炊いたご飯を天日干しした携帯用の食料であると言われています。食べる時は水に入れて食べていました。江戸時代になると、旅行者はにぎり飯を竹の皮に包んで携帯していました。また、江戸の人達は芝居見物や花見でも弁当を食べていました。芝居の幕の間に食べる

幕の内弁当

という意味で名付けられた「幕の内弁当」は今でも人気があります。

　近年、親が小さい子どもや高校生のために作るお弁当が話題になっています。日本では小学校と中学校では給食がありますが、幼稚園や高校では給食がないところが多いので、毎朝、親（主に母親）がお弁当を作ります。また、小学校でも運動会や遠足のような特別な行事の時には給食が出ませんから、お弁当を作ります。親によっては、「キャラ弁」と呼ばれるとても可愛らしいお弁当を時間をかけて作ることがあります。

　キャラ弁には色々なものが入ります。例えば、ウィンナーソーセージをタコの形にしたものがよく使われます。作り方はソーセージに切り込みを入れて、フライパンで炒めるだけなので簡単です。何が入っているかなと思いながら開けるお弁当は子ども心に楽しみなものです。また、おにぎりをパンダの形にするための道具なども市販されています。パンダの黒い部分は専用カッターで海苔を切って形を作ります。

タコウィンナー

キャラ弁

　このように可愛らしい弁当を作ってもらうと子どもは喜ぶのですが、時にはそれが競争になってしまって、親が負担に思うこともあるようです。お弁当にここまでエネルギーを使う国は他にはないかもしれません。

日本の弁当箱には材質、形状、大きさなどが違う色々な種類があります。子ども用のものは特に可愛いものが多く、大人用には保温性の高い実用的なものやデザイン性に優れているものがあります。金属製やプラスチック製の弁当箱が一般的ですが、木の板を曲げて作る「曲げわっぱ」とよばれる伝統的な木製のものを使うと和風の雰囲気を楽しむことができます。

　次に、「駅弁」は駅や新幹線などの列車の中で販売されている旅客向けの弁当のことで、鉄道の旅には欠かせない楽しみの一つです。また、最近は「空弁」と言って空港でも弁当類が売られるようになりました。

　明治時代になってから鉄道が急速に発展して、鉄道の利用者が増えました。そんな中で、1885年に初めて宇都宮駅でにぎり飯とたくあんが販売されたのが最初の駅弁だったそうです（他にも諸説あります）。

　列車内で弁当を食べること、さらには、ビールやお酒を飲むことがマナー違反にならなかったことが幸いして、駅弁は旅行の楽しみの一つとして確立しました。1970年頃までは駅弁を入れた箱を体の前に持って売り歩く販売員が駅にいて、列車が着く度にホームを歩き回って窓ごしに商売をする風景が全国でよく見られました。

　しかし、列車が高速化され窓が開かない設計になったことと、駅での停車時間が短くなったことで、ホームで駅弁を売る販売員の姿は現在ほとんど見られなくなりました。その代わりに、旅客は列車に乗る前に駅のホームで駅弁を買ったり、列車内をワゴンで回ってくる車内販売を利用したりします。沿線の名物がワゴンに乗せられているので、列車が駅に止まらなくても旅の風情が楽しめます。

車内販売

発売されてから150年、日本の駅弁は大きく進化しました。現在日本全国では2,000〜3,000種類の駅弁が販売されていると言われています。平均的な値段は1,000円前後ですが、3,000円を超える高級なものもあり

ます。地元の旬の食材を使った季節限定の駅弁も毎年たくさん発売されます。また、生石灰と水が化学反応した時に起こる発熱作用を利用して、食べる前にひもを引くと駅弁が温まる仕組みになっているものも売り出されています。

温まる弁当

　海外にも駅弁に似た弁当が買える国はあるようですが、日本ほど多くの駅弁が売られている国は他にはありません。皆さんも日本で国内旅行をする時は、旅行先だけでなく、移動中の楽しみとしての駅弁にも是非チャレンジしてみてください。

●内容質問

1　日本の弁当の起源はいつ頃だと考えられていますか。その弁当の中身は何でしたか。

2　「キャラ弁」とは何ですか。

3　「駅弁」とは何ですか。

4　元々駅弁はどうやって売られていましたか。今はどうやって売られていますか。

●発展問題

1　皆さんの国のお弁当にはどんな食べ物が入っていますか。

2　「キャラ弁」について調べてレポートして下さい。あなたはキャラ弁についてどう思いますか。

3　日本の弁当箱について調べてレポートして下さい。皆さんの国にはどんな弁当箱がありますか。

4　日本の県を一つ選んで、その県の人気が高い駅弁やユニークな駅弁を調べてみましょう。

海苔について

　寿司、おにぎり、お弁当などによく使われる海苔は和食にとって欠かすことができない食材です。海苔は海の岩について育つ藻類の一種です。ですから、生の海苔はぬるぬるしています。日本では昔から海苔を食べる習慣がありましたが、江戸時代に消費量が多くなり、東京湾では既に養殖が行われるようになっていました。当時、浅草で「浅草紙」とよばれる再生紙（和紙）が作られていました。海苔は、漁師がこの和紙作りの技法にヒントを得て、海苔を「すく」ことで現在の四角い紙のような形で作るようになったと言われています。海苔にも色々な種類があり、値段もまちまちです。良質の海苔は風味も味も格別で、安いものとは違いますから、食べ比べてみるといいでしょう。

おにぎり

ご飯を手でにぎる「おにぎり」の形は大きく4つ。三角形は関東ほか全国的で、俵型は関西、円形型は東北地方に多くみられ、球形は中部地方で爆弾おにぎりとも呼ばれています。中に入れる具材で色々な味が楽しめます。

材料（3~4人分（8個分））

ご飯	800g（米2合分）	
塩	少々	
海苔	適量	

＜具材＞

おかか：削り節	小1パック	
しょうゆ	小さじ1/2	
ツナマヨ：ツナ缶	大さじ2	
マヨネーズ	小さじ2	
塩昆布	大さじ1程度	
梅しそ：梅干し	1個	
赤しそふりかけ	小さじ1	

作り方

1　ご飯を用意する。

2　削り節にしょうゆを混ぜ、おかかを作る。

3　ツナ缶の油をきりマヨネーズを混ぜ、ツナマヨを作る。

4　おにぎり1個に対して白ごはん（約100g）を目安ににぎる。水でぬらした手に塩少々をつけて伸ばし、ご飯をのせる。具材をご飯の中央に入れて包み、好きな形ににぎる。

5　ご飯200g（2個分）をボウルに入れ、赤しそふりかけを混ぜる。1/2量のご飯に梅肉1/2個分を入れて軽く包んでにぎる。

6　海苔を巻いて出来上がり。

TIPS
・おにぎりの具材には、焼サケ、たらこ、明太子、いくらなどさまざまあります。
・手で直接にぎらず、ラップでごはんを包んでにぎることもできます。
・おにぎりはラップで包むと乾燥せず持ち運びにも便利。海苔は食べる直前に巻くとパリッとした食感が楽しめます。

第10章 給食

　「給食」は通常「学校給食」のことを指し、日本の小中学校で提供される昼食のことを意味します。現在、日本のほぼ全ての小学校とおよそ80％の中学校で昼食が給食として支給されています。費用は1食200〜300円で、給食費として家庭から集金されます。給食は学

校または地方自治体の栄養士が立てる毎月の献立表に従って調理されます。基本的に全員が同じものを食べるシステムで、食物アレルギーなど健康上の理由がない限り生徒が料理を選択することはできません[※1]。安全のために刺身やサラダなど生物が出されることはありません。また、給食が出される小中学校には食堂はなく、給食は各クラスの教室で食べます。この時、担任の教員も教室で生徒と一緒に同じ給食を食べるのが習慣です。これは日本では給食が「食育」の一環として捉えられていて、教員にとっても仕事の一部と位置づけられているからです。

　日本の学校給食は明治時代に山形県の小学校で始まったと言われていますが、現在の給食の形が確立するのは第二次世界大戦後の復興期の昭和20年代です。食糧事情が悪かった日本にアメリカの余剰小麦が支援物資として送られ、給食に使われるようになりました。その結果、米飯の代わりにパン、箸の代わりに先割れスプーンが使われていました。

先割れスプーン

　戦後のベビーブームで生まれたたくさんの子ども達が給食を通してパンを食べるようになり、その後の日本の食生活が欧米化する一因となりました。給食に米飯が戻って来るのは国産の米が余りだした1976年（昭和51年）です。現在は給食の献立も多様化し、一ヶ月の献立スケジュールには和洋中のバリエーションだけでなく日本の郷土料理や世界の各国料理をテーマにした日もあります。子ども達は

食育の一環として給食で様々な料理を味わう経験をしています。また、最近は地元でとれた食材を積極的に食べようという「地産地消」の考え方も強くなり、自分達の地域でとれた魚や野菜、そして地元で作られた味噌や醤油を給食の献立に積極的に使うという取り組みも盛んになっています。

　給食の献立は栄養士が栄養バランスを考えて作るので、基本的に健康的な料理で構成されています。しかし、子どもはどうしても魚や野菜より肉を好む傾向にあります。そこで、調理師は魚や野菜の調理方法を工夫して、栄養的にも味覚的にも子どもがおいしく食べられるような料理を作る努力をしています。

　以下は生徒数850名のある中学校の給食の流れです。この学校では、近くにある給食センターから毎日出来たての給食が届けられます。この給食センターは近隣6校の給食をまかなっていて、専門の調理スタッフが毎朝7時から4,800人分の昼食を作ります(※2)。調理が終わった給食は学校、学年、学級別に仕分けした容器に入れて、学校別のコンテナに収められて、11時頃にトラックで配送されます。

　学校ではスタッフが受け取ったコンテナから学年・学級別に分けられた容器を各階の配膳室に運びます。12時半に四時間目の授業が終わると白衣を着た給食当番の生徒5名ほどが給食を取りに来て、それぞれの教室まで運びます。

　食事の容器は教室の前方に並べられて、残りの生徒達はトレイを持って並び、順番に主食とおかずと牛乳をもらって席に戻ります。この日のメニューは洋風の献立で主食はパンでした。

全員が給食を取り終わると、生徒の代表が教室の前に出てきて「いただきます」と言って一斉に食べ始めます。担任の教員も教室にいて、生徒と一緒に同じ給食を食べます。

　食べ終わると、代表が「ごちそうさま」と言い、生徒は一人一人食器をもとのラックに返していきます。このラックはそのまま食器洗浄機に入れられるようになっていて、給食センターでの作業が効率化されるように配慮されています。スプーンの端には穴があり、大きなキーチェーンに通してスプーンの束ができるように工夫されています。生徒はスプーンを同じ向きに通していました。

　全員が同じものを食べる給食では、生徒達はいつも自分が好きなものだけを食べられるわけではありません。ですから、食育の目的は生徒達が給食を通して色々な料理、食材、味付けなどに触れる機会を与えられ、味覚の幅を広げ、発達させ、偏食を減らしていくことだと言えるでしょう。

撮影協力：鹿沼市立東中学校
撮影：畑佐一味

※１　食物アレルギーが事前に分かっている子どもの給食は除去食（アレルゲンとなる特定の食材を除いた特別食）が作られます。
※２　学校内に設置されている給食室で作る学校もあります。

●内容質問

1 日本では、小学、中学、高校、大学のどのレベルの学校で給食がありますか。

2 この中学校の給食は誰が作っていますか。また、いつ作られますか。

3 生徒は給食をどこで食べますか。教員はどこでお昼ご飯を食べますか。

4 「食育」とはどういうことでしょうか。

●発展問題

1 皆さんの国の学校では、どんなお昼ご飯を食べますか。

2 みんなが同じ物を食べる給食についてどう思いますか。

3 給食センターが一番気をつけていることは何だと思いますか。

4 日本の学校では先生も一緒に同じ給食を食べますが、これをどう思いますか。

1カップの謎

　計量カップや計量スプーンは料理をする時に欠かせない大切な道具です。ところが、国によって計量カップの大きさが少し違います。

○日本：1カップ＝200 ml

○アメリカ：1カップ＝約240 ml＝8oz

　レシピが英語で書かれている場合はアメリカのカップを使っているかもしれませんから、気をつける必要があります。

　さらに、日本でお米を炊く時に使う電気炊飯器には必ずお米の量を計るためのカップがついています。このカップは「お米カップ」とも呼ばれ、上までぎりぎりに入れても180 mlで、お米を炊く時に使う単位の「一合（ごう）」に当たります。日本酒も「合」を単位として使い、十合で一升と単位が変わるので、大きい日本酒の瓶を「一升瓶」と呼びます。「合」や「升」は容量を計るための日本の古い単位です。これに対して、計量スプーンは日本もアメリカも一緒です。

○大さじ（tablespoon）　15 ml

○小さじ（teaspoon）　5 ml

レシピ

ビーフカレーライス

学校給食でも人気のカレーライスは、日本の国民食とも言えるくらい子どもからも大人からも人気があります。野外のキャンプや合宿でよく食べるのもカレーライス。人それぞれに、いろいろな思い出がある料理です。

材料（4人分）
　ご飯（米3合）............約1kg（米450g）
　牛肉薄切り.................................200g
　人参...............................1本（150g）
　玉ねぎ.......................大1個（300g）
　じゃがいも.................小2個（200g）
　水 ....4カップ（800ml）
　カレールウ...............1パック（4人分）
　油 大さじ1
　らっきょう..............................適宜
　福神漬け..................................適宜

作り方
1　人参は皮をむいて乱切りにする。玉ねぎはくし形に切る。じゃがいもは皮をむいて3cm角に切る。牛肉は4cm幅に切る。

2　鍋に油をしいて牛肉の表面の色が変わるまで炒めたら、人参、玉ねぎ、じゃがいもを加えて2~3分炒める。

3　水を注いで沸騰させ、アクを取り、中弱火で20分煮る。

4　火を止め、カレールウを加えて溶かし、再び火にかけて5分ほど煮込めば完成。

5　ご飯を器の片側に盛り、カレーソースをかける。

6　らっきょうや福神漬けを添える。

料理のことば 乱切り，くし形に切る，○○角，アクを取る ➡ p.138

 TIPS

・市販のカレールウは、箱に入ったブロック状のほか、フレーク状のものもあります。
・ガラムマサラやクミンなど、好みのスパイスを加えてもいいでしょう。
・肉には豚肉、鶏肉はよく使いますが、羊肉を使うことはあまりありません。
・なすやズッキーニ、パプリカ等の夏野菜を入れると季節感のあるカレーになります。

第11章 郷土料理とB級ご当地グルメ

郷土料理とは、食材の保存技術や交通手段が発達する以前に人々が地域でとれた材料を使って、その土地に合った食べ方を工夫して受け継いできた地域独特の料理のことを指します。日本には北海道から沖縄まで古くから伝えられてきた郷土料理がたくさんあります。地元の産物を地元で消費することを「地産地消」と呼びますが、郷土料理はまさにこの地産地消を実践している料理です。つまり、「地元で採れた旬の素材をその土地で培われた伝統的な料理法で調理した料理」が郷土料理ということになります（『郷土料理百選』（2007年）より引用）。

農林水産省は2007年に料理研究家、食文化の有識者などの意見と、インターネットによる一般人の人気投票の結果などを基にして100の料理を選び、郷土料理百選として発表しました。農林水産省はこれらの料理を選ぶにあたり、日本全国から1,600品目におよぶ料理を候補にあげて、リストを作成したそうです。その中で一般投票数が一番多かったのは山形の「芋煮」でした。

芋煮は東北の代表的な郷土料理です。江戸時代に始まったもので、サトイモの収穫期（10月頃）に合わせて食べられていました。当時はサトイモと他の野菜だけで、豚肉や牛肉は入っていませんでした。現在も青森をのぞく東北地方で10月から11月にかけて、家族や仲間が集まってみんなで芋煮を作って食べる「芋煮会」というイベントが盛んに行われています。週末に河原に集まって行い、ちょうどピクニックのような感じです。東北地方の芋煮にはさらに細かい地域差があります。例えば、山形県の内陸中南部では牛肉と醤油を使いますが、海側など県内のそれ以外の地域では豚肉と味噌を使います。東北の他の地域では鶏肉や魚を入れる所もあります。しかし、基本的にサトイモを使うことは共通しています（三陸海岸ではジャガイモを使う所もあるそうです）。

芋煮

サトイモ

芋煮会のシーズンになると地域のコンビニなどでも薪が販売されたり、スーパーでは芋煮用の食材パックが販売されるようになります。このような光景は東北の秋の風物詩と言えるでしょう。芋煮会が盛んな山形市では、毎年9月に「日本一の芋煮会フェスティ

日本一の芋煮会フェスティバル

バル」という行事が行われます。お祭りとして行われる芋煮会の最大のもので、1989年に始まりました。会場の河原には直径6メートルもあるアルミ合金製の大鍋が用意され、建築用の重機を使って、3万食の山形風芋煮が作られるそうです。

郷土料理と似たものに、「B級ご当地グルメ」があります。「グルメ」はフランス語のgourmet（美食）で、庶民的で値段があまり高くないという意味でA級ではなくて「B級」、「ご当地」はその場所という意味です。「B級ご当地グルメ」は、古くからある郷土料理に対して、戦後に生まれて地域に根付いた料理や、地域の活性化と町おこしのために考え出された比較的新しい料理を指す言葉として使われています。特に2006年に「B-1グランプリ」というB級ご当地グルメの全国大会が開催されるようになったことが引き金になり、各地で様々な新しい料理が創作されるようになりました。料理の傾向としては焼きそばやカレー、肉料理など若い人に人気の料理が多いようです。代表的なB級ご当地グルメには、北海道札幌のスープカレー、栃木県宇都宮の餃子、静岡県富士宮の焼きそばなどがあります。

郷土料理であれ、B級ご当地グルメであれ、自分達の土地に根付いた料理について話すことは誰でも好きです。日本人と話をする時の話題作りやレストランを選ぶ時の参考にするととても便利です。また、日本国内を旅行する時には地元の料理について知っておくと旅行中の楽しみもさらに増します。

札幌のスープカレー

宇都宮の餃子

富士宮焼きそば

●内容質問

1 「郷土料理」とはどのような料理を意味しますか。

2 「B級ご当地グルメ」とは何ですか。

3 「地産地消」とはどういうことですか。説明して下さい。

4 山形の「芋煮会」はどんな行事ですか。

●発展問題

1 「郷土料理百選」を調べて中から一つ選び、レポートして下さい。

（参考 URL：https://www.maff.go.jp/j/nousin/kouryu/kyodo_ryouri/panf.html　2021.4.12 閲覧）

2 「B級ご当地グルメ」を調べて中から一つ選び、レポートして下さい。

（参考 URL：https://japan-web-magazine.com/japanese/food/index/1.html　2021.4.12 閲覧）

3 皆さんの国や地域にはどんな郷土料理がありますか。

4 あなたにとっての郷土料理は何ですか。また、子どもの時に食べた料理で、記憶に残っているものは何ですか。

わんこ蕎麦

　ソバは寒冷地で育つため、長野、北関東、東北など寒い地方でたくさん食べられるようになりました。今でも各地に有名なその土地の蕎麦があります。岩手県の盛岡市には「わんこ蕎麦」という楽しい蕎麦があります。給仕をする人が少量の茹で蕎麦をお客さんのお椀に次から次へと入れていきます。お椀が空になるとすぐ入れられてしまうので、食べ続けなければなりません。蕎麦が入れられる前にふたを閉めることができれば、終わることができます。大人の平均は 50~60 杯で、100 杯以上食べると賞状がもらえるお店があるそうです。是非、挑戦してみて下さい。

唐揚げ
からあ

唐揚げは、お弁当のおかずにもビールのおつまみにも大人気です。冷めてもおいしいのですが、外はカリッと中はジューシーな揚げたては格別です。醤油か塩か、にんにく、生姜の使い方で味付けは家庭ごとに異なります。

材料（2~3 人分）

鶏もも肉 ....1 枚（300g）
A 酒 ....大さじ 1
　 醤油 ....小さじ 1
　 塩 ....小さじ 1/3 （2g）
生姜汁（または、おろし生姜）
　 ....小さじ 1
小麦粉 ....大さじ 1
揚げ油 ....適量
レモン ....適宜

作り方

1　鶏もも肉を 4~5cm 角に切る。

2　切った鶏もも肉と A と生姜汁を混ぜて 10 分以上置く。

3　2 の鶏肉に小麦粉をまぶし、160~170℃位の低めの油で 3~4 分揚げて一旦取り出す。次に、油の温度を 180℃くらいまで上げて鶏肉をもどし、2 分ほど揚げて中まで火を通し、二度揚げする。

4　好みでくし形切りにしたレモンを添える。

料理のことば　〇〇 cm角，まぶす，二度揚げ，くし形切り ➡ p.138

 TIPS

・下味を付けた鶏肉は、冷蔵庫で一日置くと味がしみておいしくなります。

・卵白少量を鶏肉と混ぜて、少し多めに小麦粉をまぶすと、衣の厚いバリっとした食感になります。小麦粉は片栗粉でも代用できます。

・チューブのおろし生姜とおろしにんにくを使うと簡単です。好みで組み合わせてください。

第12章　食文化と価値観

　日本を訪れる外国人観光客の多くが、日本の食べ物を楽しむことをその理由の一つにあげます。また、留学や就労などで日本で生活をしている外国人、そしてその家族の数も年々増えています。必然的に複数の食文化が混在する状態が生まれ、それは日本の食文化にも影響を与えます。本章では、日本人が行ってきた食の制限の歴史を紹介し、その中から自分自身が持っている価値観に気づき、他の人の食に関する価値観に対して寛容になることを考えていきます。

　動物は草食であろうと肉食であろうと、生きるために何かを食べなければなりません。ですから、空腹になると食べても大丈夫なものは本能的に何でも食べようとして、そこに制約を設けることはしません。動物としての人間もこの例外ではありません。しかし、人間は知能が高度に発達したことで、宗教、倫理観、価値観といった本能以外の制限や戒律を作り出しました。そして、それらを「食のタブー（禁忌）」という形で実践するようになりました。

　食のタブーは世界各地に存在しますが、代表的なのは宗教に基づいたものです。ユダヤ教のカシュルートは食用動物の種類と屠畜方法に関する戒律です。イスラム教では豚は不浄な動物とされますから、豚肉は食べません。また、ヒンズー教では牛は神の使いで神聖な動物とされているので食べません。

　日本にもかつて食物に関する制限が存在しました。生き物を殺す「殺生」を禁じる仏教が大陸から日本に伝わったのは6世紀半ばとされています。13世紀に禅宗の僧侶の修行の一部として魚も肉も使わず野菜や豆などの植物性食品だけでおいしく料理を作る工夫が重ねられ、精進料理が確立しました。

　一般の庶民に向けては、7世紀に天皇が肉食禁止令を出し、その中で特定の狩りや漁をすることと牛、馬、犬、猿、鶏の肉を食べることを禁じました。日本は稲作を中心とする農耕社会でしたから、水田や畑を耕すための役畜である牛や馬を食べることは合理的ではなかったのです。8世紀以降の天皇も天候不順や自然

災害で作物の不作が心配になると、願掛けの意味で殺生を禁じ、肉食を禁止する通達を出しました。こうして、7世紀末から江戸時代の終わりまでの約1,200年間、日本人は表向きは肉をほとんど食べずに大豆製品や魚、野菜を中心とした食事をとってきました。しかし、キジや猪、鹿など野生の鳥獣肉は食べていました。また、「薬食い」といって薬という名目で隠れて肉を食べていた人はいたようです。

明治維新の後、明治政府が日本人の体格が西洋人よりずいぶん小さくて劣っていたことを危惧し獣肉食を奨励したことから、日本人の食生活は大きく変わりました。始めは、肉を食べることを「不浄」と思い抵抗感を持っていた日本人達も、徐々に牛肉や豚肉を食べるようになっていきました。

豚の角煮

精進料理は日本料理の調理法に大きな影響を与えました。お寺の近くには精進料理を出す料理屋がありますが、寺の生活を体験して精進料理を食べさせてくれる「宿坊」を利用するのもおもしろいでしょう。精進料理の中には、魚や肉の代わりにお麩や大豆製品を使って肉料理に似せる「もどき料理」があります。豆腐に野菜を混ぜて揚げた「がんもどき」は渡り鳥の雁の肉に似せて作られたものです。

精進料理

現在、日本の食材の中で国際的な議論を引き起こしているのはクジラです。日本には鯨肉（クジラの肉）を食べる習慣が12世紀頃からありました。昔は海岸に流れ着いたクジラを海からの恵みと考えて食べていたようです。その後、漁をするようになっていきました。

鯨のベーコン

イギリスやアメリカでは19世紀に鯨油を機械の潤滑油として利用するための捕鯨が行われましたが、鯨肉を食べる習慣はありませんでした。日本を含めた捕鯨国は資源を枯渇させないように捕鯨を続けたいという立場で調査捕鯨を続けてきましたが、反捕鯨国は「クジラを捕獲する」こと自体を禁止すべきだと言う立場をとっていて、相互理解が進んでいるとは言えません。

『The Cove（ザ・コーブ）』^(※1)というドキュメンタリー映画で注目を浴びた和歌山県太地町でのイルカの追い込み漁は、食用にするためとはいえ他国の文化では受け入れづらいものでしょう^(※2)。一方、地元の人にとっては「昔からの伝統の一部」であり、他文化の価値観で判断されたくないという意見もあります。

　食べていい物と食べてはいけない物という判断は人間（民族）が自ら作り出した倫理観や価値観が規定しているものであり、恣意的であると言えます。ですから、お互いの価値観を尊重し合うことの重要性は理解していても、他国の食文化を評価するのは難しい問題だと言えるでしょう。

※1　2009年に公開されたアメリカのドキュメンタリー映画。
※2　2018年には『おクジラさま―ふたつの正義の物語』というドキュメンタリー映画も製作されています。捕鯨、反捕鯨それぞれの立場をバランスよく表した作品です。

●内容質問

1 日本はいつ頃、獣の肉食が禁じられていたでしょうか。

2 「精進料理」とはどんな料理ですか。精進料理では魚は使いますか。

3 日本が国際的な議論を引き起こしている肉は、何の動物の肉ですか。

4 あなたは食に関する倫理観や価値観は恣意的であると思いますか。その理由は何ですか。

●発展問題

1 精進料理のメニューにはどんな料理があるか、調べてレポートして下さい。

2 皆さんの国の文化ではどんな食のタブー（禁忌）がありますか。

3 皆さんの国の食べ物で、他の国の人が食べないと思う物があるか調べて下さい。

4 日本の鯨漁の歴史について調べてレポートして下さい。

column
食の
ひとくち
メモ
天ぷらの衣ってなに？

　「衣」とは人の体を覆うためにつけるものを表す言葉です。「着物」「洋服」「シャツ」などはすべて衣ですから総称して「衣類」と呼びます。天ぷらでは小麦粉と卵と水を混ぜた生地（batter）で材料を覆うので「衣」と呼ぶようになりました。とんかつ、エビフライ、竜田揚げなど、揚げ物の外側についているものはすべて衣と呼びます。衣をつけないで揚げたものは「素揚げ」と呼びます。また、衣は小麦粉だけでなくアーモンドスライスなどのナッツを混ぜたりワンタンを使って作ることもできます。

　「衣がサクッと揚がっていておいしいね。」

　「この天ぷら、衣がベタベタしている。」

　「このエビフライはエビが小さいのに衣が厚くて、

　　衣ばかり食べているみたいだね。」

 肉じゃが

日本で「おふくろの味は？」と聞くと肉じゃがをあげる人が多いです。地域や家庭によって肉や味付けが違いますが、ここでは少し甘めで煮汁（にじる）多めのタイプをご紹介します。

材料（3-4 人分）

牛肉（ぎゅうにく）の薄切り（うすぎり）	....	200g
じゃがいも	....	大 2 個（約 400g）
玉ねぎ	....	中 1 個（約 200g）
人参（にんじん）	....	小 1 本（約 100g）
さやいんげん	....	5~6 本（約 30g）
油	....	大さじ 2
だし汁	....	600ml
水	....	3 カップ（600ml）
和風顆粒（わふうかりゅう）だし	....	小さじ 1
醤油（しょうゆ）	....	大さじ 2
砂糖	....	大さじ 4

作り方

1 じゃがいもは皮をむき 8 等分に切り、水につける。

2 人参は乱切（らんぎ）りに、玉ねぎはくし形に切る。

3 大鍋（おおなべ）を火にかけ油をしいて肉を入れて炒める。肉の表面の色が変わったら、人参、玉ねぎ、じゃがいもを加えて 2~3 分炒める。

4 だし汁を加えて中強火（ちゅうつよび）で沸騰（ふっとう）させ、アクを取る。

5 紙蓋（かみぶた）をして、中弱火（ちゅうよわび）で 10 分煮（に）る。

6 醤油大さじ 1 と砂糖を加えてさらに 10 分程度じゃがいもが柔（やわ）らかくなるまで煮る。

7 さやいんげんを食べやすい長さに切り、少量の塩を入れた熱湯（ねっとう）で 1~2 分ゆで、冷水に入れて冷ます。

8 仕上げに、残りのしょうゆ大さじ 1 とさやいんげんを加え、かき混ぜたら完成。

料理のことば 乱切り，くし形に切る，アクを取る，紙蓋 ➡ p.138

TIPS
· 肉は主に関東では豚肉、関西では牛肉を使います。
· 味を濃くするには砂糖としょうゆの量を増やします。砂糖としょうゆを同量にすれば甘さ控（ひか）えめの味になります。
· 煮汁（にじる）はなくなるまで煮詰（につ）めてもいいです。

第13章 ラーメン

　ラーメンは寿司と同じぐらい世界での知名度が高く、
人気がある食べ物です。中華麺がスープの中に入って
いて、上に野菜、チャーシュー(焼豚)、卵などの具材
が乗っているのが一般的な日本のラーメンです。中国
の麺料理から発展したものであることには間違いあり

醤油ラーメン

ませんが、もはや中国人も日本のラーメンは中国の拉麺(ラーミエン)とは別の物
だと認識していて、中国語では日本のラーメンを「日式拉麺」と呼び分けていま
す。ラーメンは専門店で食べるだけでなく、袋やカップに入って販売されている
インスタントラーメン(即席ラーメン)やカップ麺を自分で作って食べることでも
大変人気があります。

　ラーメンに使われている黄色の麺を日本語では「中
華麺」と呼びます。原料は小麦粉と塩で、それに「か
ん水」というアルカリ性の液体を加えて作ります。小
麦粉に含まれるフラボノイド色素がアルカリ性に反応
して黄色く発色し、中華麺独特の色と香りを作り出し

中華麺

ます。かん水は元々モンゴルから来たものですが、中国にはかん水を使わない麺
もたくさんあります。

　日本全国には約26,500店ほどのラーメン店があります(「iタウンページ」(https://itp.
ne.jp/)(2020)調査より)。ラーメンの歴史は明治時代に入ってから始まり、函館の「養
和軒」という店が「南京そば」という料理を出したのが日本のラーメンの最初の
記録のようです。東京では1910年に浅草で初めてのラーメン専門店「来々軒」が
出来ています。その後全国に広まっていったのですが、この頃は「ラーメン」と
いう呼び方はまだなく、日本蕎麦と区別するために、「支那そば」とか「中華そば」
と呼ばれていました。

　中国語の「拉麺」は「引っ張って作る麺」という意味ですが、日本のラーメン

はうどんや蕎麦と同じで「切って」作るので正確には「拉麺」とは言えません。「ラーメン」という名称の語源は諸説あるのですが、札幌の竹屋食堂が始まりという説が有力です。竹屋食堂は1921年に北海道札幌市の北海道大学の近くに出来ました。元々、普通の食堂だったのですが、1922年に中国人の料理人を迎え「支那料理・竹屋」となりました。北海道大学には中国からの留学生もいたので、店は繁盛しました。その時の人気メニューは塩味の「支那そば」でした。しかし、オーナーの奥さんが「支那そば」という名前が差別的で好きではなく、違う名前を考えていた時に、料理人が料理ができた時に大声で言う「ハオラー（好了）」という言葉の「ラー」と「麺」を繋いで「ラーメン」という呼び方を作ったそうです。

　20世紀に入って中華料理店は順調に増えていくのですが、1923年の関東大震災で多くの店が壊滅的な打撃を受けました。しかし、震災からの復興のために料理屋の料理人が屋台でラーメンを出したり、東京以外で営業するようになり、全国的に広がっていきました。第二次世界大戦後もラーメン店は増加の一途を辿りました。

ラーメンの屋台

　そして、1958年に熱湯をかけて3分待つだけで食べられる即席ラーメン「日清チキンラーメン」が初めて発売されました。この商品名によって「ラーメン」という呼び方が全国的に広まり定着しました。さらに、1971年には日清食品が即席ラーメンをカップに入れたカップ麺、「カップヌードル」という商品を発売し、その手軽さとおいしさから爆発的に売れました。カップ麺は1989年に袋入りのインスタントラーメンの売り上げを上回り、世界中の国々でも売られるようになりました。それに伴い味の種類も増え、今ではトムヤンクン風味などエスニック系のカップ麺も登場しています。

即席ラーメン　　カップ麺

日本には「新横浜ラーメン博物館」のようにラーメンをテーマにした娯楽施設があります。テーマレストランと呼ばれるこのような施設では、日本各地の人気ラーメン店の味を一度に試すことができます。また、「札幌ラーメン横丁」のようにラーメン店が一つの場所に集中しているところが日本各地にあります。昔は醤油味、塩味、

札幌ラーメン横丁

味噌味だけだったラーメンですが、豚骨スープ、鶏ガラスープ、カツオやイワシを使った魚介スープなど味のバリエーションが増えています。麺も太い麺から細い麺、まっすぐなストレート麺やちぢれ麺など店ごとにこだわりがあり、さらに茹で方も硬いものから柔らかいものまで頼むことができる店もあります。

味噌ラーメン

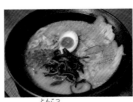
豚骨ラーメン

太麺

細麺

スープをかけずに麺につけて食べる「つけ麺」や、油のたれを麺に混ぜて食べる「油そば」も最近人気です。

中国から入ってきた料理が日本でアレンジされ、もはや中国人にさえも中華料理とは認識されなくなってしまった日本のラーメン。色々なラーメンに挑戦して、是非、「自分の一杯」を見つけて下さい。

つけ麺

油そば

●内容質問

1 日本のラーメンの麺はどのように作りますか。

2 日本のラーメンは、広まり始めた頃何と呼ばれていましたか。

3 日本の「ラーメン」の語源は何ですか。

4 「即席ラーメン」と「カップ麺」はそれぞれいつ頃作られましたか。

●発展問題

1 日本でおもしろいラーメンのお店に行ったことがありますか。どんなお店でしたか。

2 皆さんの国にはどんなラーメン店がありますか。

3 皆さんの国に、日本のラーメンのように、元々外国から来た料理が大きく変化したものが
あるか調べてみましょう。

4 今人気があるラーメン店について、インターネットで調べて、どんなラーメンかレポート
して下さい。

食べログのラーメンランキング（https://tabelog.com/ramen/rank/ 2021年4月12日閲覧）
ラーメンデータベース（https://ramendb.supleks.jp 2021年4月12日閲覧）

ラーメンのことば

　日本のラーメンは種類がとても多いので、ラーメンの用語を知っていると、
店を選んだり、注文をしたりする時に役に立ちます。

麺を表す言葉	太麺　細麺　ストレート麺　ちぢれ麺
スープを表す言葉	醤油　塩　味噌　豚骨　豚骨醤油　鶏ガラ 煮干し　魚介　白く濁ったスープ　透き通ったスープ 背脂多め / 普通 / 少なめ
トッピング	チャーシュー　メンマ　ナルト　野菜炒め　コーン 味付玉子・味玉・煮玉子・半熟玉子　ねぎ　海苔 ほうれん草
味を表す言葉	あっさり　こってり　まろやか　コク　風味　うま味
茹で方	ばりかた　かため　ちょいかた　ふつう ちょいやわ　柔らかめ
卓上での風味付け	胡椒　おろしにんにく　酢　ラー油

煮たまご入りラーメン

ラーメンのトッピングとして人気の煮たまごは、家庭で簡単に作れます。黄身のトロッとした半熟加減と醤油ダレに漬け込む時間で味わいが変わります。煮たまごを作って、家で本格的なラーメンを作ってみましょう。

●煮たまご

< 材料 >

卵	5~6 個
A 醤油	大さじ 3
酒（白ワインでも可）	大さじ 2
砂糖	大さじ 1

< 作り方 >

1 鍋にたっぷりの湯を沸騰させる。卵を入れて 8 分ゆでる。

2 鍋から卵を取り出し、すぐに水で冷やす。殻をむき、ビニール袋に卵を入れて A を加える。空気をできるだけ抜いて袋の口を閉じる。

3 冷蔵庫で 6 時間置くと食べごろ。冷蔵庫で 2~3 日は保存できる。

●煮たまご入りラーメン

< 材料（1 人分）>

麺（冷凍、またはインスタント）	1 食分	煮たまご	1 個
湯	300ml	ねぎ、ナルト、メンマ	適宜
A 鶏ガラスープの素	小さじ 1		
醤油	大さじ 1		
こしょう	少々		

< 作り方 >

1 お湯と A を鍋に入れて温め、ラーメンスープを作る（市販の麺についたスープも可）。ねぎ、ナルト、メンマなどトッピングするものを切っておく。

2 別の鍋で麺をゆでる（記載のゆで時間に従う）。

3 器に熱々に温めた 1 のスープを入れ、麺を湯を切って入れる。半分に切った煮たまごとその他トッピングをのせる。

料理のことば 湯を切る ➡ p.138

 TIPS
・煮たまごで大事なのは、卵のゆで時間をしっかり測ることです。7分半だと黄身の中央が流れるくらいの固さで、8分半だと流れない固さになります。

・煮たまごはタレに漬けて長く置くとしょっぱくなります。長時間置くときは酒を大さじ3に増やしましょう。

第14章 うなぎ（鰻）

うなぎは「蒲焼き」にして食べるのが一般的です。うなぎの蒲焼きは寿司、天ぷら、蕎麦とともに江戸時代にできた江戸の四大料理の一つです。全国に約2,800店ほどのうなぎ料理店があり（「タウンページデータベース」(2011)より）、日本中どこでも食べることが出来ます。

鰻重

2000年頃までは、日本は世界のうなぎの生産量の約7割を消費していましたが、現在は中国をはじめアジア諸国での日本食ブームにより日本以外での消費量が大きく増加しました。

ウナギは千年以上前から日本で食べられていましたが、現在のように人気がある食べ物になったのは江戸時代で、「蒲焼き」という調理法ができてからです。うなぎの蒲焼きは串に刺したウナギに醤油とみりん、砂糖などで作ったタレをつけて炭火の上で直に焼いた料理です。醤油の焦げるにおいは食欲をそそるので、蒲焼きを焼くときのにおいだけでもご飯が食べられるという話が落語に出てきます。

うなぎ

醤油にみりんや砂糖を混ぜて作り出される味は「甘辛」と呼ばれます。すき焼きや牛丼も甘辛の味付けですし、照り焼きチキンの味も甘辛です。日本で砂糖が生産されるようになったのは江戸時代のことです。また、江戸時代後期にこいくち醤油が千葉県の野田、銚子でたくさん作られるようになったおかげで、この甘辛の味が生まれました。甘辛のタレが川魚であるウナギの泥臭い匂いを隠し、蒲焼きのタレとウナギの相性がとても良かったことが、うなぎの蒲焼き人気を高めたと考えられます。

蒲焼き

ガマの穂

「蒲焼き」という言葉の語源は、15世紀にウナギをそのまま開かずに切って串に刺して焼いた形が「ガマ（蒲）の穂」に似ていたことが始まりだとする説が有力です。元の発音は「がまやき」で、それが訛って「かばやき」となったそうです。その後、ウナギを割いて開いた身に串を刺して焼く現在の形に変化しましたが、今でも「蒲」の字を使い、「蒲焼き」と呼ばれています。

日本では毎年7月の終わりの決まった日にうなぎを食べる習慣があります。その日は「土用の丑の日」と言われる日で7月の後半に来ますが、毎年同じ日になるとは限りません。その日が近くなると今年は何日が「土用の丑の日」かしらと気にして、うなぎの蒲焼きを食べるのを楽しみにする人がたくさんいます。しかし、実はうなぎは年間を通していつでも食べることができ、その旬は冬です。それなのに、日本での消費量が最も多い月は7月です。下のグラフは2002年のうなぎの蒲焼きの月別支出割合と日別支出割合を表しています。圧倒的にその年の土用の丑の日だった7月20日にうなぎの蒲焼きへの支出額が増え、よく売れたことがわかります。

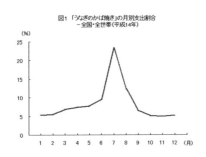

図1「うなぎのかば焼き」の月別支出割合
－全国・全世帯（平成14年）

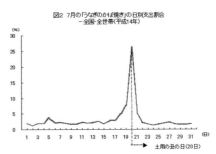

図2 7月の「うなぎのかば焼き」の日別支出割合
－全国・全世帯（平成14年）

（総務省統計局（2002）より）
http://www.stat.go.jp/data/kakei/topics/topics04.htm

「土用の丑の日」にうなぎをよく食べる理由には諸説あるのですが、一番有力だとされているのは、江戸時代後期に夏にうなぎが売れなくて困っていたうなぎ屋から相談を受けた平賀源内という学者が、「夏の暑い時期（土用）にうなぎを食べると夏バテ防止になる」という宣伝案を出したからとするものです。この宣伝が大

成功して、夏の暑い時期にうなぎを食べる習慣が定着したそうです。

　うなぎは栄養価が高い食べ物だという認識はもっと古くからあったという記録があります。例えば、万葉集（8世紀）の中に歌人の大伴家持がうなぎについて詠んだ和歌が二首収録されています。

　石麻呂に　吾物申す　夏痩せに　良しといふ物ぞ　鰻漁り食せ
（俺は石麻呂に言ってやった。夏痩せにはうなぎがいいらしいから、獲ってきて食べなさい。）

　痩す痩すも　生けらばあらむを　はたやはた　鰻を漁ると　川に流るな
（げっそり痩せても生きていられればいいんだから、万が一にでもうなぎなんか獲りにいって、
川に流されるなよ。）

　これは大伴家持が友人の吉田石麻呂に対して詠んだ和歌です。石麻呂はとても痩せた人だったそうで、一首目では、うなぎを獲って食べて、元気になりなさいと言っています。しかし、二首目では、痩せてはいても生きていられればいいんだから、うなぎを獲ろうとして川で流されてはいけませんよとからかっています。二人はとてもいい友達だったのでしょう。江戸時代に「土用の丑の日」にうなぎを食べることを提案した平賀源内もこの和歌のことを知っていたのかもしれません。
　日本で消費されているうなぎの99％は養殖です。養殖のためには、体長5cmほどのうなぎの稚魚（シラスウナギ）を網で捕獲し、養殖場で一年半ほど育てます。しかし、近年、稚魚の漁獲量が激減しており、資源確保の努力をしなければならない状態になっています。

●内容質問

1　日本ではいつ頃からうなぎを食べていた記録がありますか。

2　「甘辛」はどのような味のことですか。

3　「蒲焼き」の語源を説明してください。

4　「土用の丑の日」はいつですか。現在、その日にうなぎを食べるようになった理由の一説は何ですか。

●発展問題

1　日本以外の国にはどんなうなぎの料理があるか調べて、レポートして下さい。

2　蒲焼きのタレのような味は好きですか。同じようなタレを使った他の料理について、調べてみましょう。

3　どうしてうなぎの値段は高くなってしまったのですか。

4　うなぎを絶滅させないためにどのような努力がなされているか調べてみましょう。

column
食の
ひとくち
メモ

関西と関東の蒲焼きの違い

　関西ではうなぎの蒲焼きを作るとき、腹開きにしたうなぎに串を打って、タレにつけながら炭の直火で念入りに焼きます。一方、関東ではうなぎを背開きにし、串を打ったら、まず、何もつけずに直火で焼きます。次に40分ほど蒸して、余分な脂を落として身を柔らかくします。そして、最後にタレをつけながら直火で焼いていきます。関東のうなぎの蒲焼きの食感は身が柔らかくてフワフワしています。それに対して、関西の蒲焼きは身がしっかりしていてカリカリしています。どちらもおいしいので、食べ比べてみて下さい。

　関東でうなぎを背開きにするのは、江戸は武士の町で「切腹」を嫌ったからとする一説がありますが、それはあまり信憑性がないようです。うなぎの場合、背開きにするほうが技術的に簡単で、そのほうが速かったとする説のほうが有力だと言われています。

<ruby>レシピ</ruby>

<ruby>親子丼<rt>おや こ どん</rt></ruby>

「親」はニワトリ、「子」はタマゴ、両方を<ruby>組<rt>く</rt></ruby>み<ruby>合<rt>あ</rt></ruby>わせた<ruby>丼<rt>どんぶり</rt></ruby>です。<ruby>砂糖<rt>さとう</rt></ruby>と<ruby>醤油<rt>しょうゆ</rt></ruby>の<ruby>甘辛<rt>あまから</rt></ruby>い味付けは、<ruby>好<rt>この</rt></ruby>みで<ruby>調味料<rt>ちょうみりょう</rt></ruby>の量を<ruby>加減<rt>かげん</rt></ruby>して下さい。とても人気がある<ruby>丼<rt>どんぶり</rt></ruby>の一つです。

材料（2人分）

<ruby>鶏肉<rt>とりにく</rt></ruby>（もも肉）	....	160 g
玉ねぎ	....	大 1/2 個（約150g）
卵	....	3 個
三つ葉	....	1/2 束
だし汁	水	250ml
	<ruby>和風顆粒<rt>わ ふう か りゅう</rt></ruby>だし	小さじ 1/4
砂糖	....	大さじ 2
<ruby>醤油<rt>しょう ゆ</rt></ruby>	....	大さじ 1
<ruby>七味<rt>しち み</rt></ruby>、<ruby>粉山椒<rt>こ さんしょう</rt></ruby>	....	<ruby>適宜<rt>てき ぎ</rt></ruby>

作り方

1 玉ねぎは皮をむき、半分に切って 5mm 幅に切る。鶏肉は 2cm 角に切る。三つ葉は 3㎝の長さに切る。

2 卵をボウルに割り、ほぐす。

3 <ruby>鍋<rt>なべ</rt></ruby>にだし<ruby>汁<rt>じる</rt></ruby>、砂糖、醤油を入れて<ruby>中<rt>ちゅう</rt></ruby>～<ruby>強火<rt>つよ び</rt></ruby>にかける。<ruby>沸騰<rt>ふっとう</rt></ruby>したら、玉ねぎを入れて 2~3分<ruby>煮<rt>に</rt></ruby>る。

4 鶏肉を加えて 2~3 分煮る。鶏肉に火が通ったら、<ruby>溶<rt>と</rt></ruby>き卵をまわし入れ、三つ葉を加える。

5 <ruby>蓋<rt>ふた</rt></ruby>をして 20 秒ほど加熱したら火を止める。<ruby>余熱<rt>よ ねつ</rt></ruby>で卵が<ruby>半熟<rt>はんじゅく</rt></ruby>に仕上がるように火を通す。

6 ご飯を<ruby>丼<rt>どんぶり</rt></ruby>によそい、5 を上にのせ<ruby>煮汁<rt>に じる</rt></ruby>をかける。

7 <ruby>好<rt>この</rt></ruby>みで<ruby>七味<rt>しち み</rt></ruby>や<ruby>粉山椒<rt>こ さんしょう</rt></ruby>をかける。

料理のことば ○○cm 角, ほぐす, まわし入れる, 余熱, よそう ➡ p.138

TIPS ・ 卵に完全に火を通す場合は、5の加熱時間を長くする。

・ 三つ葉は<ruby>独特<rt>どくとく</rt></ruby>の香りがある<ruby>香草<rt>こうそう</rt></ruby>。パセリなど、他のハーブに変えてもよい。

第15章 お好み焼き

　穀物を挽いて粉にしたものを調理して食べることを「粉食」といい、世界中に粉食文化が存在します。日本では粉が主材料の料理を「粉もの」または「粉もん」と呼び、うどん、蕎麦、ラーメン、ワンタン、パスタ、ピザ、トルティーヤ、チヂミなどはすべて粉ものにあたります。また、ケーキ、ドーナツ、パンケーキ、クレープなど甘い粉ものもあります。本章では日本の代表的な「粉もの」として人気のある「お好み焼き」「たこ焼き」「もんじゃ焼き」を紹介します。

お好み焼き：

　お好み焼きの発祥は16世紀の茶人、千利休が作った「麩の焼き」という茶菓子だと言われていますが、現在のお好み焼きは1930年代に東京の屋台で売られていたものが原型になっているようです[※1]。それが大阪に伝わって、広まっていきますが、第二次世界大戦で中断

関西風お好み焼き

されてしまいます。しかし、戦後の復興期に復活し、ウスターソースよりも粘度の高い濃厚なソースを使って、現在の関西風のお好み焼きが出来上がりました。関西風のお好み焼きは「混ぜ焼き」と言われ、刻みキャベツ、肉、エビ、イカなどの具材と小麦粉の生地(batter)を混ぜ合わせて鉄板の上でパンケーキのように焼きます。裏返して両面を焼き、お好み焼き用のソースと、好みでかつお節、青のり、マヨネーズをかけて出来上がりです。フワフワの軽い食感を出すためにすりおろした山芋を入れることもあります。また、お好み焼き店では客席のテーブルに鉄板が組み込まれていて、客が自分で焼くお店もあります。

　広島風のお好み焼きは、戦争で焼け野原になった広島でお好み焼きを作る屋台が数多く現れたところから始まりました。食糧難の時代で材料を集めるのも大変な時代に地元の食べ物として育ちました。広島風の特徴は「乗せ焼き[※2]」である

ことです。始めに、小麦粉の生地を鉄板の上に薄くク
レープのように伸ばします。そこにせん切りのキャベ
ツを15cmくらいの高さになるほど山盛りに乗せ、豚
肉、エビ、イカなどの具材を重ねていきます。そして、
全体をひっくり返してキャベツを蒸し焼きにします。

広島風お好み焼き

その後、卵など他の具材を足して、最後にお好み焼きソースを塗り、青のり、刻
みねぎ、マヨネーズなどをかけて出来上がりです。広島風お好み焼きの店で客が
自分で焼くことはありません。

たこ焼き：

　　たこ焼きは1930年代に大阪で考案されたもので、関
西の庶民の味を代表するソウルフードと言えます。

　　小麦粉を水、あるいは、出汁に溶かした生地を半球
形の型にあふれるくらい入れ、一つ一つにタコを入れ
て、鉄串でくるくると回しながら、生地をボールのよ

たこ焼き

うに丸く焼いていきます。最後にたこ焼きソース、かつお節、青のりをかけて出
来上がりです。外がカリカリで中が熱くてトロトロな食感になります。それを爪
楊枝や竹串で刺して食べます。1960年代には関東でも屋台販売が行われるように
なりました。それに伴い、全国的にも広がり、お祭りなどの縁日で出る屋台の定
番になっていきました。さらに、1990年代にはテイクアウトを中心にしたたこ焼
きチェーン店が現れ、現在はほぼ日本全国どこででもたこ焼き店が見られるよう
になりました。また、家庭でも手軽にたこ焼きが作れる「たこ焼き器」が市販さ
れているので、たこ焼きパーティも子どもや若い人達の間では人気があります。

たこ焼きの屋台

家庭用たこ焼き器

もんじゃ焼き：

　もんじゃ焼きは1800年代の始めに江戸で生まれました。元々、子ども達が水に溶いた小麦粉で鉄板の上に文字を書き、焼いて食べた「文字焼き」という食べ物でした。浮世絵で有名な葛飾北斎が『北斎漫画』(1819年)の中で描いた絵が残っています。江戸時代末期から明治時代にかけては、駄菓子屋の一角で子ども達が自分で作れる食べ物として広まっていきました。「もじやき」が訛って、「もんじゃやき」と呼ばれるようになりました。もんじゃ焼きは、お好み焼きに比べると、小麦粉に対しての水の量が多く、ソースや醤油を先に混ぜて生地に味をつけてから焼きます。具材はキャベツ、肉、魚介類が中心ですが明太子、餅、チーズなども入れたりします。また、もんじゃ焼きは基本的に客が自分で焼きます。みんなでワイワイ言いながら、コテと呼ばれる小さなヘラを使って生地を鉄板に押し付けて焼いて食べるのがもんじゃ焼きの楽しみ方です。

もんじゃ焼き

コテ

※1　1938年に開店した古いお好み焼き屋「風流お好み焼き　染太郎」が今でも浅草で営業しています。古民家のようなとても味わいがあるお店です。

※2　「重ね焼き」とも言います。

●内容質問

1　お好み焼きにはどんな具材が使われますか。

2　大阪と広島のお好み焼きの違いは何ですか。

3　「たこ焼き」はどのように全国に広まっていきましたか。

4　「もんじゃ焼き」の名前の語源（ごげん）は何ですか。

●発展問題

1　大阪のお好み焼きに「モダン焼き」というのがあります。どんなお好み焼きか調べてみて下さい。

2　広島には「〜ちゃん」という名前のお好み焼き店が多くあります。その理由を調べて、レポートして下さい。

3　日本の甘い粉（こな）ものにはどんなものがあるか、調べてみて下さい。

4　世界には様々な粉食文化が存在しますが、どのようなものがあるか調べてレポートして下さい。

column
食の
ひとくち
メモ

「ねかす」って寝（ね）かす？

　「ねかす」は「子どもを寝（ね）かす」などのように、「眠らせる」が本来の意味ですが、調理の途中で「合わせた材料や調味料をしばらく置いておく」という意味でもよく使われます。ねかすことで味がなじんだり、柔らかくなったり、コシが生まれたり、発酵（はっこう）するなどの効果があります。材料によって冷蔵庫に入れる、ラップをかける、濡（ぬ）らしたふきんなどで包んでおくなど、ねかせておく状態は異なります。カレーなども一晩（ひとばん）ねかすと味がなじんでおいしくなるといいます。また、白身で身質がかたいタイなどの魚は活（い）けじめにしてすぐ食べるよりも1〜2日ねかすことで熟成（じゅくせい）が進み、身の中のうま味成分が増えておいしくなると言います。つまり、刺身（さしみ）の味は鮮度（せんど）だけで決まるわけではないのです。牛肉をドライエイジング（dry aging）という方法でねかすと肉が熟成（じゅくせい）してよりおいしくなるのと同じ変化です。

お好み焼き

ソースとキャベツ、薄力粉、卵さえあれば、好きな具材を組み合わせて自分の好きな「お好み焼き」が作れます。自分なりのオリジナルお好み焼きのレシピを見つけてください。

材料（2~3人分）

＜生地＞

薄力粉	50g（大さじ5強）
水	60ml
和風顆粒だし	小さじ1/2
卵	1個
天かす	大さじ3（約10g）
すりおろし山芋（長芋）	大さじ1~2
油	小さじ1

＜具材＞

豚薄切り肉	5~6枚（50g）
キャベツ	2~3枚（100g）

※シーフード、牛肉、焼きそば、チーズ、キムチ、明太子、餅、紅しょうが、青ねぎなど

＜ソース・トッピング＞

お好み焼きソース	大さじ2
削り節	小さじ1程度
青のり	小さじ1/2程度
マヨネーズ	適宜

作り方

1　大きめのボウルに水、顆粒だしを入れ、薄力粉を加えて混ぜ、生地を作る。

2　キャベツを3~4mm幅にきざむ。

3　1にキャベツ、卵、天かす、すりおろし山芋を加えて混ぜる。

4　フライパンを火にかけ、油をしき、豚肉を並べて、その上に3をのせて広げる。厚さは好みで1.5~2cmくらいにする。

5　蓋をして中弱火で4~5分焼く。裏返して3~4分焼く。

6　お好み焼きソース、削り節、青のりをふりかける。マヨネーズは好みでかける。

TIPS　・山芋、または長芋は、皮をむいてすりおろします。入れなくても作れます。

　　　・とんかつソース、中濃ソースでも代用できます。

　　　・「お好み焼き粉」という商品も市販されています。

めしあがれ
MESHIAGARE

食文化で学ぶ上級日本語

A Culinary Journey through Advanced Japanese

English Translation

Chapter 1 Japanese Food Culture

Japan is situated between the northern latitudes of 45° and 20° (equivalent to Maine–Florida on mainland U.S.A. and from northern Italy in Europe to Morocco in Africa) and it is made up of more than 6,500 islands, including the four main islands of Hokkaido, Honshu, Shikoku and Kyushu. Most of Japan is located in the temperate zone, thus enjoying four distinct seasons, with just Hokkaido in the subarctic zone and Okinawa in the subtropics.

Approximately 75% of the land is mountainous, with tall ranges more than 3,000 meters high running through the center of the country. There are many rivers, water is plentiful, and water quality is high. Further, because both warm and cold currents flow in the coastal waters, Japan has some of the most bountiful fishing grounds in the world. For these reasons, Japan has a rich supply of seafood, vegetables and meats, and the people can savor the blessings of both the mountains and seas. Japanese people have long benefited from this favorable climate and topography, sourcing an array of ingredients to use in cooking. The distinguishing features of the food culture this gave rise to are outlined below.

The first fundamental principle of Japanese food culture is to accentuate the innate flavor of each ingredient. Chefs do very little to ingredients, working to maximize the natural aromas, flavors and textures of each one. Sashimi is a prime example of this. In *washoku,* Japanese cuisine, if fish is fresh, the preference is always to serve it raw. When not as fresh, fish is heated and served in grilled or simmered dishes. Of course, in the past, only those living near the coast could enjoy raw fish, but apparently even those living in the mountains considered sashimi the best way to eat fish. This strong tradition for eating raw foods in Japan spurred advancements in technology to preserve perishable foods, and consumers grew very sensitive to the freshness of ingredients. This may be one reason Japan has gained global recognition for its food safety standards.

The second principle is the custom of experiencing the shifting seasons through food. Japan has four distinct seasons and ingredients change with the seasons. In

82

addition, certain foods are closely associated with
annual rituals and festivals. Throughout the year,
the period in which a particular fish or vegetable is
at its most delicious is called *shun*, meaning season.
The yellowtail season, for example, is in winter,
when catches are large and flavors are especially
delicious. Winter yellowtail even has a special name—*kanburi*. For Japanese people,
its appearance in supermarkets signals winter's arrival. October is the season for
chestnuts; when October comes around, you can find all kinds of chestnut dishes
and showcases are filled with Japanese and Western-style chestnut sweets. The seasons
have become less obvious with the advent of refrigeration and freezing technologies,
however, seasonal awareness continues to drive ingredient selection in *washoku* course
meals, such as the formal banquet style *kaiseki ryori*. Restaurants of French and Italian
cuisine also serve dishes based on seasonal ingredients. Seeing ingredients through the
lens of seasonality allows for deeper enjoyment of Japanese eating habits.

Flexibility around food is the third feature of Japanese food culture. The Japanese
tend to have very little resistance to incorporating foreign customs for living into
their daily lives. Ordinary households make Japanese, Western and Chinese dishes,
and those of many other countries for their daily table. And such dishes appear
repeatedly. Japanese value tradition but also adapt well to new things. As seen at
the time of the Meiji Restoration, a wave of rapid Westernization gave birth to
Japanized forms of Western foods, including *tonkatsu* breaded pork cutlet and *kare
raisu* curry with rice, creating a new category that came to be known as *yoshoku*.

The final key feature of Japanese food culture is the importance of rice. Rice is
said to have been introduced to Japan from the Asian continent approximately 3,000
years ago, after which rice cultivation began locally. Westernization of the Japanese
diet since the end of World War II has led to a decline in rice consumption, but
rice remains an important staple food today. Rice has also played a role beyond
mere foodstuff throughout Japanese history. In ancient times rice equated to wealth
and was thus used in offerings to gods and to pay taxes, and samurai salaries were
paid in rice. In modern Japan too, it holds a status
above mere agricultural crop, as seen in its frequent
use at ceremonies and festivals in the form of mochi
pounded rice, sake rice wine, cooked rice and ears of
rice grains. Rice cultivation is even protected under
agricultural policies.

 # Tempura

You can enjoy a variety of seasonal ingredients as tempura if you learn good techniques for making the batter and frying. Tempura is great with *tentsuyu* dipping sauce, but also delicious with a variety of specialty salts, like matcha salt.

● Ingredients（serves 2）

<Tempura ingredients >
2-4 unshelled prawns
4 thin slices of kabocha pumpkin
2 small fresh shiitake mushrooms
1 small eggplant
2-4 green beans
2 *shiso* perilla leaves
Vegetable oil

<Tempura batter >
1 tbs beaten egg
100 ml iced water
120 ml (approx. 70g) cake flour

<Tempura dipping sauce >
200 ml water
1/4 tsp powdered Japanese soup stock
1 tbs each of dark-colored soy sauce and mirin
3 tbs finely grated daikon

● Directions

1 Shell prawns leaving tails attached. Cut the tips off the tails. Insert several cuts into the belly and press gently to straighten prawns. Thinly slice pumpkin. Cut eggplant into quarters and insert vertical cuts. Remove the shiitake stems and carve a cross into each cap. Cut green beans in half. Wash shiso leaves and pat dry.

2 Place all tempura dipping sauce ingredients into a small saucepan and bring to a boil. Grate daikon, drain excess liquid, and set aside.

3 To make the tempura batter, mix beaten egg with iced water. Sift flour into mixture in equal amounts to the liquid ingredients (approximately 120 ml). Use chopsticks to mix roughly leaving dry flour lumps in the batter.

4 To a deep frying pan, add oil to about 70% capacity and heat to 170°C.

5 Lightly coat tempura ingredients with flour (extra), dip in batter and fry in oil. Raise oil temperature to 180°C just before removing ingredients.

TIPS Other excellent tempura ingredients include white-fleshed fish fillets, squid, chicken, *renkon* lotus root, onion, sweet potato, asparagus, zucchini, seaweed, and all kinds of mushrooms.

To make iced water, add ice to water and discard ice once cooled.

For tempura batter using one whole egg, use 200-400 ml of iced water. Less iced water will result in light batter, while more will result in a firmer, crunchier batter.

For store-bought Japanese noodle soup base, simply dilute with water before serving.

Chapter 2　Kanto and Kansai Regional Cuisine - A Comparison

Even slight variations in where you were raised in a country give rise to cultural differences. These can manifest as pride in your own region or a sense of competition with others. Such regional differences exist in every country: in the US, it is the North and the South or East Coast versus West Coast; in Australia it is between Victoria and Queensland; and in the UK, it is across the four major regions. In China, the differences between north and south in ingredients and seasonings are immense. In Japan's case, the biggest division is usually between Kanto and Kansai—the regions around Tokyo and Osaka, respectively. The disparities in food culture, in particular, are striking.

The clearest examples of different food culture across Kanto and Kansai can be seen in two cooking basics— dashi soup stock and soy sauce. Nowadays, you find both everywhere, but historically Kansai cuisine has been based on dashi extracted from kombu kelp (kombu dashi), while the main variety in Kanto has been bonito

Kombu　　　Bonito flakes

dashi (*katsuo* dashi). Kombu is a type of seaweed that grows in the cold ocean waters of Japan's north. From the Muromachi period (1336–1573) through the Edo period (1603–1868), kombu harvested in Hokkaido was transported by boat on the Sea of Japan to present-day Fukui Prefecture. It then passed along Lake Biwa before following a land route to Kyoto. The result was the establishment of *Kyoryori* Kyoto Cuisine based on kombu dashi with dishes seasoned in a way that accentuates the mild flavor of kombu dashi. In contrast, bonito is a fish caught and processed into flakes on the Pacific Ocean side of Japan, and its use gained widespread popularity in Edo (present-day Tokyo). Bonito dashi is distinguished by a stronger flavor than kombu dashi. Both dashi types have subsequently come to be used across Japan, and a common modern form known as *awasedashi* combines stock drawn from both kombu and bonito for more concentrated umami.

Soy sauce is the most important fermented seasoning at the Japanese daily table. Koji mold spores (*Aspergillus oryzae*) are added to soybeans and wheat to make a

Soy sauce

starter mixture called koji to which brine is then added. The preparation is allowed to rest and mature for six months or sometimes more than one year. Fermentation takes place in the presence of koji mold, yeast and lactic-acid bacilli, resulting in soy sauce. This method combines soybeans and wheat, but some varieties of soy sauce are made entirely from soybeans.

The prototype for soy sauce was a seasoning transmitted from China in the 8th century. From there Japan developed its own unique fermented seasonings starting with miso. The origin of soy sauce is actually in the liquid that seeps out in the miso-making process. And that is the earliest form of what is now called tamari soy sauce.

In the 17th century, early in the Edo period, two different styles of soy sauce came about in Hyogo Prefecture (Kansai) and Chiba Prefecture (Kanto). In the beginning, Kansai had very large production volumes and the sauce was shipped

Usukushi shoyu *Koikuchi shoyu*

to Edo, but production volumes increased in Kanto by the late Edo period. Both styles involved fermenting a combination of brine and a koji base of soybeans and wheat. However, the Kansai-style sauce was light in color with a lighter flavor, and was therefore called *usukuchi shoyu*, or light-colored soy sauce. Kanto soy sauce, in contrast, was dark in color and had stronger flavor, earning it the name *koikuchi shoyu*, or dark-colored soy sauce. The dark and light refers simply to the variation in color; in terms of salt content there is virtually no difference.

These differences can still be seen in modern cuisine in both regions. Most fish consumed in Kansai is caught in the near coastal waters of the Seto Inland Sea, has white flesh and is mild in flavor. The most common of these is *tai* sea bream. Seasoning with light-colored soy sauce and kombu dashi enhances the innate flavors and results in beautifully colorful cuisine. Dark-fleshed fish like bluefin tuna and bonito caught in the Pacific Ocean feature more in Kanto. The richer

■Typical Sashimi Varieties   ■Udon and Soba Noodle Soups

 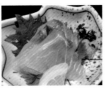  

| Kanto: dark-fleshed fish | Kansai: white-fleshed fish | *Koikuchi shoyu*-based in Kanto | *Usukuchi shoyu*-based in Kansai |

flavor of the flesh pairs better with the more aromatic dark-colored soy sauce and bonito dashi. These differences can also be seen in *mentsuyu* noodle soups of the two regions. Kansai-style udon soup uses *usukuchi shoyu* and is therefore very light in color, whereas the noodle soups of Kanto have a darker color because of the *koikuchi shoyu* used to flavor them. Both styles are delicious and definitely worth trying.

There are many other interesting differences between Kanto and Kansai. Several of the most well-known are shown below, and we recommend you try some of these and discover the differences yourself.

	Kanto	Kansai
● *Inari-zushi* (vinegared rice in seasoned deep-fried tofu pockets): triangles in Kansai, but cylinders (modelled on *tawara* rice sacks) in Kanto.		
● *Nigirimeshi* (rice balls): in Kanto, called *onigiri*, shaped like triangles and made with roasted seaweed. In Kansai, called *omusubi*, shaped like rice sacks and wrapped in seasoned seaweed.		
● *Ozoni* (New Year's dish): in Kanto, flavored with soy sauce and typically served with rectangular mochi. In Kansai, miso-flavored with round mochi.		
● *Negi* (green onions/ spring onions): Kanto uses white spring onions with a larger white portion, whereas Kansai typically uses green spring onions with a large proportion of green.		

Tsukimi Moon-Viewing Soba in Kanto-style Soup

A whole egg in the soup alludes to the full moon.

Kanto has a soba culture, whereas Kansai has an udon culture. The color of Kanto-style soba noodle soup is dark, with strong soy sauce flavor. The enjoyment of Kansai udon soup, in contrast, is more in the umami-rich and salty dashi flavor.

● Ingredients（serves 1）

1 serving soba (dried noodles)
1 egg
400 ml water
A | 1/2 tsp powdered Japanese soup stock
   | 2 tbs dark-colored soy sauce
   | 1 1/2 tbs mirin
Green onions, for garnish

● Directions

1　To make the noodle soup, place the water and all ingredients in A in a small saucepan and bring to a boil.

2　Fill a separate saucepan with plenty of water, bring to a boil and add dried noodles, cooking according to instructions on the package (takes 7-8 minutes on average).

3　Transfer 150 ml of the noodle soup from step 1 into a small lidded saucepan and turn heat on. Crack egg into the soup and put lid on for 30 seconds to 1 minute then remove from heat. Cook to desired firmness with residual heat.

4　Finely chop green onions.

5　Drain the boiled noodles in a colander and place in serving bowl. Reheat soup from step 1 and pour the hot soup over noodles. Top with egg from step 3 and garnish with green onions.

TIPS　Best to eat noodles immediately. If boiled soba noodles are allowed to sit they become soft and limp (*soba ga nobiru*, literally "the soba noodles stretch").

A sprinkling of *shichimi togarashi* seven spice mix is a delicious touch.

For store-bought Japanese noodle soup base, dilute with water according to instructions for warm noodle soup (*kake tsuyu*).

Chapter 3 Dashi and Umami

Dashi is often described as "the lifeblood of *washoku*," showing its importance in Japanese cooking. Flavorful dashi is indispensable in delicious cuisine. The origin of the word dashi is *nidashijiru,* which is defined as an "umami-rich broth made by extracting flavor from dried bonito, kombu kelp and other ingredients" (Digital Daijisen, accessed 2021.4.10). Typical ingredients used for dashi in Japanese cooking include kombu, dried bonito flakes, dried sardines, and dried shiitake mushrooms. Dashi brings an umami component to cooking, enhances flavor, and plays the role of accentuating the overall taste of a dish.

Umami is now recognized as one of five flavors that can be sensed chemically by the human tongue, but this is a relatively recent development in the West. Conventional Western ideas of taste included only four elements—sour, sweet, salty and bitter(※). The discovery of umami through research into glutamic acid found in kombu by chemist Kikunae Ikeda in 1908 led to its addition as the fifth element of taste, and umami subsequently became known around the globe in the late 1980s. The Japanese word umami takes two forms which determine the English translation and notation: it means "good flavor" or "delicious taste" if it contains the character 旨 meaning "delicious," but it is used directly as "umami" when referring to the fifth taste element.

The stocks and soups of Western and Chinese cuisine can be broadly referred to as "dashi." Base ingredients such as meats, seafood and vegetables are simmered for a long time to extract flavor. Much umami is extracted in this process, however, the complex layers produced by many other flavor components make it difficult to taste umami standalone. In contrast, the features of dashi in Japanese cuisine are the use of foods such as dried bonito flakes and kombu, and the short amount of time required to extract flavor. Very little else besides the umami component of bonito flakes and kombu is extracted, making it possible to taste the full flavor of

Kombu, dried shiitake
bonito flakes, dried sardines

umami when drinking Japanese dashi. Adding a small amount of salt before serving makes the umami more intense. The umami we experience can be divided into three broad categories of glutamic acid, inosinic acid and guanylic acid. Kombu contains large amounts of glutamic acid, bonito flakes and dried sardines are full of inosinic acid, and dried shiitake mushrooms are rich in guanylic acid. Dashi stocks combining various umami components result in a stronger sense of umami.

Kombu

Kombu is a variety of seaweed found in the cold ocean waters of Hokkaido and the Tohoku region. Sometimes growing up to three meters long, kombu is harvested and sun-dried before being sold in dehydrated form. Storage of dried kombu leads to decreased astringency and the emergence of a flavor similar to sweetness. This flavor is glutamic acid—the umami component of kombu. Currently, more than 90% of Japan's kombu is produced in Hokkaido. During the Edo period (1603–1868), kombu was transported by *kitamae-bune* cargo vessels connecting Hokkaido and Osaka via the Hokuriku region on the western sea route. The availability of large volumes of kombu in western Japan gave shape to a kombu dashi culture. The cargo boats also exported kombu to China via Satsuma (present-day Kagoshima Prefecture), and because they made stopovers in the Ryukyu Kingdom (present-day Okinawa Prefecture) kombu usage also spread there (see map on website). To this day there are many regional Okinawan dishes based on kombu.

In the ocean

Sun-drying

Dried kombu

Dried bonito

Katsuobushi is dried bonito made through a process of simmering, smoking and drying bonito flesh. A variety known as *honkarebushi* takes the process further by fermenting the flesh after it has been treated with a particular type of mold. Similar processed foods exist in coastal areas where bonito are caught, such as the Maldives, however the fermented

Honkarebushi

90

dried bonito style of *honkarebushi* can only be found in Japan. With just 15% water content, these blocks of dried bonito that look like wood chips at a glance are thought to be the hardest food in the world. In fact, the Japanese name for bonito (*katsuo*) is said to derive from *katauo* meaning "hard fish," and it seems Japanese people have been drying the fish for food preservation since long ago.

The dried bonito we know today was first produced in Kishu (present-day Wakayama Prefecture) in the 15th century, and by the Edo period, good-quality dried bonito was being made in Tosa (Kochi Prefecture), Satsuma (Kagoshima Prefecture), Yaizu (Shizuoka Prefecture) and other regions.

At dried bonito factories, the flesh is first sliced into three pieces before being slowly simmered in hot water. The pieces are then smoked and dried in a repeated process that causes the moisture to evaporate and flesh to harden. Next, mold is applied and the flesh is dried further to remove even more moisture. The process takes several months and results in very hard dried bonito that is filled with the umami component inosinic acid.

In order to make dashi from dried bonito, it first needs to be made into thin shavings. In the past, each household shaved the precise amount of flakes they needed every day themselves, but this is no longer necessary now that packs of dried bonito shavings are readily available in supermarkets.

※ The flavor element "spicy" experienced through pepper, chili peppers and wasabi, among others, is a type of physical stimulation, not chemical stimulation, and is thus not included as one of the tastes recognized by the tongue.

Dashi-maki Tamago (Rolled Omelet)

Japanese-style omelet is frequently found in bento lunch boxes and is especially popular among children. The *dashi-maki tamago* style introduced here is a favorite accompaniment to sake at soba restaurants.

● Ingredients

3 eggs
4 tbs water (60 ml)
1/4 tsp powdered Japanese soup stock
A | 1/4 tsp soy sauce
  | 1 tsp mirin
  | pinch of salt
1 tsp oil
Finely grated daikon
Soy sauce

● Directions

1 Crack eggs into a bowl and use a cutting action through egg whites to mix roughly.

2 Dissolve powdered soup stock in water and add to the mixture in step 1. Add seasonings in A and mix.

3 Place an omelet pan over medium-low heat and add oil. Use a small piece of paper towel to spread the oil thin and remove excess.

4 Pour one-fifth of the egg mixture into the pan and roll the mostly cooked egg from the back of the pan towards the front.

5 Slide the rolled egg to the back of the pan, add a little oil at the front, and repeat the process in step 4 until all egg mixture is used.

6 Remove omelet from pan and place on a cutting board. Cut crosswise into bite-sized pieces and serve on a plate.

7 Garnish with a mound of grated daikon seasoned with a few drops of soy sauce.

TIPS An omelet pan is a small rectangular frying pan. This recipe can also be made in a round frying pan, however, it will not have uniform thickness.

Adding 2 tbs of sugar results in a sweet omelet (*atsuyaki tamago*). Adjust sugar amount to desired sweetness.

Chapter 4 Sushi

One category of *washoku* that enjoys unwavering popularity is sushi, widely recognized as delicious cuisine in places all over the world. So much so that the name "sushi" is used as is, requiring no further explanation. However, sushi does not only come in the style shown in the photo at right; many different varieties of sushi can be found around Japan.

Nigirizushi

The most likely explanation for the etymology of the word sushi is in *sushi meshi*, meaning "sour rice." And while there are several theories for the origin of the dish itself, the most commonly understood one is that sushi was created as a preserved food around 3 BCE by Southeast Asian farmers who wanted to make fish last longer. Fish were pickled with salt and cooked rice for several months to undergo lactic acid fermentation. When the process was complete, farmers rinsed off the rice which had dissolved into a thick liquid and ate only the fish.

This food preparation process was introduced to Japan via China. A 9th century record of preserved fish called *narezushi* is said to mark the beginning of sushi in Japan. Fish, salt and rice were pickled together over several months but the rice was washed away and only the fish flesh was eaten. Even now, the legacy of *narezushi* endures in a Shiga Prefecture dish called *funazushi*. Around the 14th century, there emerged a variety of sushi dishes intended to be eaten with rice with names such as *namanare* and *izushi,* and these still feature in regional cuisines around Japan.

Funazushi

New styles called *hakozushi* and *oshizushi* were developed in the Kansai region during the Muromachi period (approx. 1336–1573). Salted fish and rice were either pressed into a box or shaped into blocks and pickled. These are considered the earliest forms of modern-day styles known as *Osakazushi* and *sabazushi* (pickled mackerel sushi).

Oshizushi

Early in the Edo period (1603–1868), vinegar production methods were established, thus enabling mass production. And in the 17th century, this gave rise to a new form of sushi called *hayazushi* based on rice with vinegar mixed through it, replacing the previous method for adding acidity through lactic acid fermentation. The first store to make this style, known as *sasamaki-kenukisushi,* is still open for business in Tokyo today.

Then in the early 19th century, *nigirizushi* was invented by Edo sushi chef Hanaya Yohei (※1). This style is now commonly referred to as Edomae sushi(※2) and it is the model for the cuisine that is now globally recognized as sushi. Just like modern food trucks, stalls at that time served a variety of foods, including tempura and even *nigirizushi*. As there were no storage facilities like refrigerators, sushi in those days consisted of vinegared rice topped with seafood prepared to avoid spoilage through methods such as boiling (boiled *hamaguri* clam and boiled conger eel), pickling in vinegar (gizzard shad), and marinating in soy sauce (*maguro* tuna lean red flesh). Those marinated in soy sauce were known as *zuke* and some modern sushi restaurants still serve *maguro* marinated in this way.

Amusements While Waiting for the Moon on the Night of the Twenty-sixth in Takanawa, a Famous Place in the Eastern Capital by Utagawa Hiroshige (Ota Memorial Museum of Art Collection)

With the development of ice-making technology in the Meiji period (1868–1912) fish could now be refrigerated. While sushi was fundamentally a dish of the Kanto region at the time, it spread nationwide in part owing to one major event—The Great Kanto Earthquake of 1923. The disaster caused enormous damage in Tokyo and chefs who had been working at Tokyo sushi restaurants returned to their hometowns. With sushi chefs scattered all over the country, Edomae sushi became available nationwide.

Photo cooperation: Sushi Isshin (Asakusa)

By the 1950s, sushi restaurants had earned a very expensive image. But then the *kaitenzushi* sushi train style appeared in the 1960s when an Osaka sushi restaurant installed a conveyor belt and customers helped themselves to sushi that revolved in front of them. The style grew popular because of the clear and affordable pricing system with bills calculated based on the number of plates taken. Modern sushi train restaurants are diversifying their menus and now serve a variety of dishes like ramen and desserts in addition to sushi.

Kaitenzushi sushi

When the 1980s came around, sushi was no longer confined to Japan. It had gained broad attention and popularity overseas and was referred to simply as sushi. And just as the Japanese have adapted Western cuisine to suit their tastes, innovative sushi styles have emerged around the globe. One of the most well-known is the "California roll." Characterized by seaweed rolled on the inside, the variety apparently was an answer to a general American distaste for seaweed on the outside. This style is now known as *ura-maki*, or inside-out rolls. Also popular overseas are sushi rolls containing a number of different ingredients. What kind of sushi do you have in your country?

California roll

※1 Various theories exist on the inventor of *nigirizushi*, but in this book we have adopted the theory crediting Hanaya Yohei.

※2 Edomae originally meant "the sea in front of Edo," namely Tokyo Bay, and "Edomae sushi" originally referred to sushi made with ingredients sourced in Tokyo Bay, but today it refers broadly to the style of *nigirizushi*.

Samon Chirashi-zushi (Salmon Scattered Sushi)

Scattered sushi, known as *chirashi-zushi,* is a popular homemade dish for Hinamatsuri Girls' Day celebrations. Once you learn how to make sushi rice, you can enjoy all kinds of variations with a wide range of toppings at home.

● Ingredients (serves 2)

150 g short-grain rice
(makes approximately 350 g of sushi rice)
<Sushi Vinegar>
1 1/2 tbs rice vinegar (or grain vinegar)
1 tbs sugar
1/4 tsp salt
<*Kinshi-tamago* omelet threads>
1 egg
1 tsp sugar
a pinch of salt
a little oil
50 g smoked salmon
50 g crab sticks
2-3 snow peas
Toasted seaweed, for garnish

● Directions

1   Cook rice slightly firm (for rice cookers, use slightly less water than indicated by line marker on bowl).

2   Prepare sushi vinegar by dissolving sugar and salt in vinegar.

3   Prepare sushi rice by pouring sushi vinegar over freshly cooked hot rice and mixing evenly. Set aside to cool.

4   To make *kinshi-tamago* omelet threads, add sugar and salt to egg and mix well. Heat a frying pan with a small amount of oil and pour mixture in, tilting pan to spread and cook thinly and evenly. Remove from pan. Once cooled, cut the thin omelet into fine thread-like pieces.

5   Boil snowpeas in lightly salted water for about 1 minute. Transfer to iced water to preserve color.

6   To assemble, place sushi rice on serving platter and top with small pieces of cut or torn seaweed and *kinshi-tamago*. Scatter the smoked salmon, crab sticks and snow peas.

TIPS   *Chirashi-zushi* always contains omelet threads, but feel free to choose other toppings as you please.

Chapter 5　The Origin of Yoshoku

Outside Japan, the phrase "Kobe beef" is commonly used to signify premium steak, and people even talk about "wagyu" raised in Australia. However, it is not that long ago that Japanese people started eating beef.

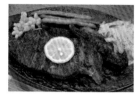

Steak

In the second half of the 19th century when the Meiji Restoration brought an end to Japan's policy of national isolation, an order for Westernization prompted the rapid introduction of Western culture. The Japanese government felt a sense of crisis at the diminutive Japanese physique compared to Westerners and encouraged people to eat meat, eggs, milk and other dairy products. A 7th century imperial order prohibiting the consumption of animal flesh in Japan meant that for approximately 1200 years Japanese people did not raise cattle, pigs or poultry for meat. No matter how much the government encouraged them, Japanese people were simply not accustomed to eating these foods. They found it difficult and many apparently worried that eating meat would dirty their bodies. It was against this backdrop that a beef hot pot dish emerged, and that was the beginning of today's sukiyaki.

Sukiyaki

By the time the 20th century began, many dishes emerged adapting Western cuisine to Japanese tastes starting a new genre called *yoshoku*, meaning "Japanized Western cuisine." In this book, we take a deeper look at two of the most typical such dishes that remain popular today—*tonkatsu* and *kare raisu*.

Tonkatsu Breaded Pork Cutlet

This dish is made by coating pork in flour, beaten egg and then breadcrumbs before deep-frying. The most common cuts of pork are the loin and fillet. Pork loin contains quite a lot of fat whereas fillet is lean and tender. The *katsu* part of the name comes from *katsuretsu*, which is the Japanese pronunciation of the French word *cotelette* (cutlet in English). And the Japanese character for pig can be read as *buta* or *ton*, thus *tonkatsu* is a coined word mixing Japanese and French. In the early Meiji period (1868–1912), Western-style eateries called the dish *poku katsuretsu* (pork cutlet) and served it with a knife and fork.

Tonkatsu

Poku katsuretsu was originally prepared with relatively thin meat fried in a small amount of oil. However, around 1930, frying a thick steak-like piece in plenty of oil yielded a new style that was hearty and tender. And it was served in pre-cut pieces so people could eat it with chopsticks. This brought about the style of *tonkatsu* treated as a *washoku* dish that we see today, served with shredded cabbage, miso soup, pickles and a bowl of rice. A sauce made to pair with the dish was invented and this so-called *tonkatsu sosu* can be found at supermarkets everywhere.

Kare Raisu Curry with Rice

Another typical *yoshoku* dish is curry with rice. It is one of the most popular dishes among Japanese for both home-cooked meals and dining out. Statistics from the All Japan Curry Manufacturers Association suggest that Japanese people eat curry on average between 60 and 70 times a year, showing its integral role in the Japanese diet.

Kare raisu

In India, the birthplace of curry, dishes and soups contain many spices, but not a single food resembles Japanese-style curry. Further, the word "curry" does not even exist in India. The word is thought to originate in the colonial period as the English interpretation of either "kari" from the Tamil language meaning rice topped with soup, or the Hindu word "turcarri" meaning fragrant thing.

Curries were introduced to England in the 17th century and adapted to European flavors. However, as people were not accustomed to mixing numerous spices for each dish, a company called Crosse & Blackwell created and commercialized a spice mixture called curry powder in the late 18th century.

Curry powder arrived in Japan via England during the Meiji period, and the prepared curry was served with cooked rice and initially called *raisu kare* (rice curry). Flour was added to curry powder to thicken the dish which was offered at Western-style restaurants as haute cuisine.

In the early days, Japan relied on imported curry powder, but then locally made curry powder appeared in 1920, after which came the development of curry cubes that could be added to simmered meat and vegetables, thereby simplifying the cooking process.

Curry powder

Curry cubes

This gave rise to a wide range of uniquely Japanese curry dishes: soba restaurants started serving dishes blending Japanese and Western cuisine like *kare nanban* and *kare udon* (curry-flavored soup with soba or udon noodles, respectively), and bakeries put curry inside bread dough and deep-fried it to make *kare pan*. In the 1950s, a variety of curry cube flavors (and varying spice levels) hit supermarket shelves. Towards the end of the 1960s, retort pouch curry was sold, representing the world's first-ever commercial boil-in-the-bag dish. Curry with rice went on to permeate regular households at an incredible pace.

Kare pan

Kare udon

Tonkatsu (Breaded Pork Cutlet)

Shredded cabbage is the standard accompaniment for *tonkatsu* and many specialty restaurants offer all-you-can-eat cabbage. *Tonkatsu* is a great bento dish, and also delicious simmered in a soy sauce-based soup with egg and served on top of rice as *katsu-don*.

● Ingredients （serves 2）
  2 thick slices of pork (loin or fillet)
  3-4 tbs (approx. 40 g) flour
  1 egg
  1 cup *panko* breadcrumbs (dried or fresh)
  Vegetable oil
  2 cabbage leaves
  Lemon, tomato and parsley, for garnish
  Tonkatsu sauce
  Mustard paste

● Directions
1 With a knife, make several incisions through the connective tissue between the meat and fat.

2 Beat egg in a bowl. Coat pork first with flour, then egg, and finally *panko* breadcrumbs.

3 Fill a frying pan with oil to 3-5 cm depth and heat to 160-170°C. Put pork from step 2 into the oil and fry for 2 minutes. Turn over and fry for a further 2 minutes, then remove from pan.

4 Raise the oil temperature to 180°C and return pork to oil to fry for another 1-2 minutes until golden brown.

5 Finely shred the cabbage leaves. Serve pork with cabbage, lemon, tomato, parsley, hot mustard and *tonkatsu* sauce.

TIPS   Adjust cooking time according to thickness of meat. When especially thick, fry for 3-4 minutes on each side.

Cuts of meat are named differently in each country. In Japan, loin is called *rosu* and *hire* means fillet.

 Chapter **6** Rice

Rice is one of the three most common grains on earth alongside wheat and corn. Approximately 90% of the world's rice is produced and consumed in Asia. China is the largest producer, followed by India.

Rice is the grain harvested from the *Oryza sativa* plant, which has two main subspecies—Indica and Japonica. The grains of Indica rice are long and narrow (long-grain rice), stay separate with no stickiness when cooked, and are thus used in dishes where rice is mixed with other ingredients. Indica rice is often found in Southeast Asian and Indian cuisine. In contrast, Japonica rice grains are short (short-grain rice) and sticky when cooked. The Japanese call cooked white rice *shiro gohan,* and it is custom to combine it with other dishes to achieve *kochu chomi,* a method of eating to enjoy changing taste sensations inside the mouth.

Varieties of both Indica and Japonica rice can be categorized as table rice or glutinous rice. Plants producing Japonica table rice in Japan are grown in flooded paddies. The method helps mitigate damage caused by continuous cropping and is the reason why you see rice being grown in the same paddies year after year. Table rice cultivars include Koshihikari, Akitakomachi and Hitomebore. The most popular of these is Koshihikari, comprising approximately one-third of all rice grown in Japan. Glutinous rice is used to make mochi, sticky rice cakes. One other type of rice under cultivation is *shuzomai,* used to make the alcoholic beverage sake.

When Japanese rice is cooked it appears glossy. It has a plump, tender and sticky texture and releases more sweetness as it is chewed. The flavor does not change even when cooled, so it can be enjoyed as *onigiri* rice balls, sushi, and in bento lunch boxes. Rice is without question the staple food of the Japanese, and the dishes served alongside cooked rice are called *okazu*. When Japanese people come across a dish that goes well with white rice, they compliment it saying, "I can't stop eating rice!" A key concept in *washoku* Japanese cuisine is *ichiju sansai,* meaning a meal of "one soup, three dishes." Rice is so central to every meal that it is not even mentioned in the concept name.

Rice is said to have been introduced to Japan from the Asian continent around the 9th to 10th century BCE. Well-suited to Japan's climate of plentiful rainfall in the early summer rainy season and high temperatures and long hours of sunlight in summer, cultivation of the crop spread nationwide. Remains of rice cultivation in paddies from the Yayoi period (300 BCE–300 AD) can be found all over Japan. In one anecdote of Japanese legend, when a goddess came down to earth from her abode in Takamagahara (the Shinto heavens), she came bearing rice. This shows

Ichiju sansai

how the idea of rice as a special item bestowed by the gods has existed in Japan since ancient times. In various modern-day rituals, offerings of rice, sake and salt are prepared as expressions of gratitude to the gods. Foods offered to gods at shrines are called *shinsen*, and typically include rice-based products such as rice grains, ears of rice, cooked rice, mochi and sake. In homes with family Buddhist altars, it is custom to present a small offering bowl of rice called *buppanki* as food for one's ancestors.

Clearly an important foodstuff since long ago, the long-term storage potential also made rice a symbol of wealth. A growing perception that large rice stores translated as wealth made rice important economically, too. In the Middle Ages rice was used for taxes. In the Edo period (1603–1868), farmers settled their land tax with rice, samurai salaries were paid in rice, and common units of measurement related to rice quantities, such as *hyo* (sack) and *koku*,

Buddhist altar offerings

equivalent to about 180 liters and considered enough rice to feed one person for a year. However, rice was not the only grain eaten even by farmers engaged in its cultivation; it was common to eat rice mixed with millet and other assorted grains.

Rice cultivation is more carefully safeguarded by the Japanese government than any other crop. Japan's overall food self-sufficiency rate stands at just 40% but is 100% for the staple food rice (2018 Ministry of Agriculture, Forestry and Fisheries estimate), and rice is the only crop for which domestic production covers consumption. However, recent diversification in food has drawn attention to the issue of a shift away from rice consumption among the Japanese. Efforts are being made to offset this trend by increasing rice consumption through school lunches, for example.

Tori Gomoku Meshi
(Rice Cooked with Chicken and Vegetables)

Takikomi gohan—rice cooked with various ingredients—is a typical rice dish that people associate with the taste of home. Each family has its own flavor with different ingredients and seasonings. Diverse variations range from chicken and vegetables with soy sauce flavor to a simple salt-flavored *mame gohan* rice containing green peas or other beans.

● Ingredients (serves 4)

300 g medium-grain rice
<Main components>
120 g chicken thigh meat
40 g carrot
30 g *gobo* burdock root
30 g bamboo shoots (packed in water)
40 g konjak jelly
20 g *abura-age* thin deep-fried tofu
20 g *shimeji* mushrooms
20 g enoki mushrooms
390 ml water

A | 2 tbs sake
  | 1/2 tsp salt
  | 1 tbs soy sauce

Green onions, for garnish

● Directions

1　Wash rice thoroughly then soak in water for 30 minutes. Transfer to a colander to drain.

2　Scrub the burdock root. With the burdock root on the cutting board, make several vertical slits (about 5mm in depth) rotating the burdock 90 degrees between each slit. Next, with your knife at a 45-degree angle, shave off thin layers. Rotate the burdock root while shaving. (This cutting technique is called *sasagaki*.) Soak shavings in water. Cut konjak into rectangular strips and boil 2-3 minutes. Place *abura-age* in a dish and pour boiling water over to remove oil. Cut into rectangular strips.

3　Cut carrot into quarter-circle slices and bamboo shoots into matchsticks. Remove hard base from mushrooms. Cut chicken into 1 cm cubes.

4　In a heavy pan, place rice from step 1, the water, and seasonings listed in A. Top with ingredients from steps 2 and 3.

5　Put the lid on and turn heat on to medium-low for 7-8 minutes until it starts to boil. Do not remove the lid during heating. Reduce heat to low once it is boiling and steam starts to emerge from around the lid. Cook for 12-15 minutes, being sure to remove the pan from the heat as soon as all the water is absorbed and no more steam emerges. Leave lid on to steam for 10 minutes. If you smell burning before the first 12 minutes passes, immediately turn off heat and steam for 10 minutes.

6　Remove lid and fold all ingredients together. Serve in rice bowls topped with finely chopped green onions.

TIPS　The basic ratio of ingredients to rice for this dish is between 1:1 and 1:2. For rice cooked with peas/beans (*mame gohan*), use 50 g of beans for every 100 g of rice. When combining various ingredients as in the above recipe, use a total of 100 g of ingredients for every 100 g of rice.

You can use a vegetable peeler to make burdock shavings instead of the *sasagaki* cutting technique in step 2.

Chapter 7 Chopsticks

Chopsticks are an eating implement used mostly in the countries of East Asia, including Japan. The oldest record of their use is from China in the 14th century BCE, and it is thought they were introduced to Japan along with Buddhism around the 6th century. The famous Chinese historical text *Records*

of the Three Kingdoms contains an account of Japan called *Gishiwajinden,* which notes that Yayoi period (300 BCE–300 AD) Japanese people were eating with their hands. Currently, approximately 30% of the world's population eats with chopsticks, a further 30% uses knives and forks, and the remaining 40% occupy a food cultural sphere in which eating with hands is the norm.

Even among countries that use chopsticks, variations in their food cultures have given rise to minor differences in the forms and applications of chopsticks. For example, Chinese chopsticks are longer than Japanese ones and do not have pointed tips, and they are often used in combination with a spoon that has a deep, flat bowl. The reason for this seems to be the custom of Chinese cuisine in which individuals serve themselves from large platters. Korean chopsticks are thin, made from metal and used in combination with a long metal spoon. In China and Korea, where these spoons are used to scoop up soups and liquids, it is poor manners to bring a bowl to one's mouth to drink directly from it.

Korean metal tableware

In contrast, the use of spoon-like implements did not take hold in Japan where the custom is to eat only with chopsticks. As a result, bowls holding miso soup and other broths are picked up and brought directly to the mouth for drinking. In order to cool down hot liquids, people blew on or sucked in air with them giving rise to a culture of slurping. This is thought to be the reason for tolerance

today toward the noises created when slurping. In addition, bowls did not get too hot and were likely easy to pick up because they were typically made from wood. With regard to chopsticks, Japanese have served whole grilled fish at the table since long ago, and chopsticks with thin, pointed tips made it easier to pull away the flesh and remove small bones. Chopsticks can also be used to grasp small items and cut through soft foods. However, as it is poor etiquette to stab food with chopsticks to eat, practice is required for picking up slippery or soft foods.

A variety of chopsticks exist with different applications. The most typical are chopsticks for personal use at the daily table. In Japanese households each member of the family has their own designated chopsticks and rice bowl and it is custom to eat with them at each meal. Individual chopsticks may be made from wood, bamboo, plastic or other materials and range from cheap to very expensive. One of the most beautiful varieties is *nuribashi*, chopsticks produced with traditional lacquering techniques. Chopsticks also come in many cute designs, so it is a great idea to visit a chopsticks specialty store and find your own special pair.

Other types include cooking chopsticks called *saibashi*, *toribashi* used for serving oneself from platters, and single-use *waribashi* for parties or supplied with bento boxes. These are just some of the varieties of chopsticks and the purposes they serve.

There is important etiquette when it comes to chopstick use and here we present three key items to remember. First, never stand chopsticks in a bowl of rice. This is called *tatebashi* and is a custom reserved for funerals in which chopsticks are stood upright in a bowl of rice offered to the deceased. Second, do not pass food directly from one person's chopsticks to another. Called *awasebashi* or *hashiwatashi*, this is considered very bad manners. Third, it is not appropriate to use *chigaibashi* or chopsticks that are mismatched in size or material. In Buddhist custom after the deceased is cremated, proper etiquette requires chopsticks of different lengths to be used to pick up the bones which are then passed from chopstick to chopstick. Using chopsticks in ways that are reserved for situations related to death is considered inauspicious and poor etiquette.

Chopstick rests called *hashioki* are small tableware accessories used to ensure the tips do not touch the table. From the traditional to the unique, it might be fun to explore the countless styles of chopstick rests and start your own collection.

Miso Soup

Miso soup is the perfect pairing for cooked rice. With different types of miso soybean paste and ingredients within, the variations are endless. The base soup stock can be made from dried sardines, dried kombu or bonito flakes, each offering different flavor profiles. The dish is easy to make but has great depth.

● Ingredients（serves 2）

600 ml dried sardine dashi
　　700 ml water
　　20 g dried sardines
3 tbs miso soybean paste
1 block (approx. 300 g) tofu
3 tbs dried wakame seaweed
1 green onion

● Directions

1　Remove heads and innards from dried sardines and place in a pot with the water.

2　Turn on heat. When it comes to a boil, reduce heat to low and simmer for 10 minutes. Use a colander to drain, saving the liquid stock.

3　Put dried wakame in water to rehydrate.

4　Cut tofu into 1.5 cm cubes. Finely chop green onions.

5　Place the stock from step 2 in a pot and turn on heat. When it has come to a boil, add tofu and wakame. Return to a boil and turn off heat.

6　Add miso and dissolve in the dashi. Turn heat on again and when soup is hot, add the green onions and then serve in individual bowls.

TIPS　Popular miso soup ingredients: tofu, thin deep-fried tofu, wakame, long onion, onion, daikon, potato, taro, and *shijimi* and *asari* clams.

You can preserve the delicious dashi and miso flavors by making sure the soup does not reach a fast boil after the miso has been added.

When using powdered soup stock, be careful not to add too much. The role of dashi is fundamentally to enhance the other flavors in a dish.

Chapter 8　Japanese Noodles - Udon and Soba

Noodles are long and thin and made from a dough of wheat or rice flour mixed with water and salt. In Western cuisine, perhaps the most famous type of noodle is Italian pasta. In China, Vietnam, Cambodia, Thailand, and other countries of Asia, a wide variety of noodles are consumed. The most well-known Japanese noodles are udon and soba, and they represent some of the most popular foods in Japan.

Udon

To make udon, wheat kernels are ground into flour and combined with water and salt, although some varieties do not contain salt. The resulting dough is kneaded before being rolled out flat and cut into strips. The most likely explanation for the origin of udon is that it was introduced around the 8th century by an envoy to Tang China. In the Goto Island archipelago of Nagasaki

Prefecture, a port of call for the envoy, an old style of udon called Goto Tenobe Udon still exists today. Until the Edo period (1603–1868), udon was a precious food item not widely consumed by commoners. That is because production of udon depended on a stone mill for turning wheat into flour. Stone mills were originally used to make matcha fine powdered green tea, and because there were limited numbers, they did not make their way into regular people's hands. That all changed during Japan's Sengoku period from the late 15th century to 16th century. Feudal lords across Japan began building castles and stonemasons gathered from around the country to construct the stone walls. Incredibly busy with castle-building at first, the stonemasons gradually found free time, which they used to make stone mills. The more readily-available stone mills facilitated mass production of flour, and by the Edo period, udon had become a popular food for commoners too. Unlike rice, wheat was not subject to taxation, so after the annual rice harvest farmers would use the same land to grow wheat for their own supplies.

　Thus, udon spread throughout Japan in the Edo

Stone mill

period and unique versions of udon still exist in every corner of the country today. These include Inaniwa Udon in Akita Prefecture, Oshibori Udon in Nagano Prefecture, Ise Udon in Mie Prefecture and Goto Udon from Nagasaki Prefecture.

Udon noodles come in varying levels of thickness and softness. The word used to describe the firmness of udon is *koshi*. To say udon has *koshi* means it is firm yet elastic when chewed. This firmness is lost with overboiling, causing udon noodles of any kind to become soft and limp. Because Ise Udon from Mie is boiled for a long time, it is a style distinguished as soft and lacking *koshi*.

 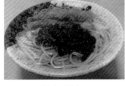 

| Inaniwa Udon | Goto Udon | Ise Udon |

Perhaps the most famous of Japan's udon styles is Sanuki Udon from Kagawa Prefecture, known for its very firm noodles. Kagawa is the smallest prefecture and has a population of just one million, but it boasts the highest per capita consumption of udon in Japan. Said to have as many as 900 udon eateries, Kagawa has earned the nickname "Udon Prefecture," with some locals even known to eat udon for breakfast. At Takamatsu Airport, which serves Kagawa Prefecture, a faucet dispenses udon soup free for everyone to drink!

Soba

Soba's history in Japan is longer than that of udon with buckwheat already under cultivation for its seeds in the country approximately 9000 years ago during the Jomon Period (14000–300 BCE). Compared to rice, buckwheat can grow in less fertile soils and can withstand dry and cold weather, making it a very hardy crop. However, because the seeds of buckwheat are harder than rice, soba was not widely eaten until the Edo period.

With stone mills more readily available in the Edo period, buckwheat flour could now be produced in large quantities as with wheat flour. The earliest buckwheat flour dish was not the thin soba noodles we know today; rather it was a dish of simmered dumplings called *sobagaki*. In the early 17th century, kneaded buckwheat flour dough was rolled out and cut into thin strips to make a dish called

sobakiri—the original form of the soba noodles we eat today. The Edo period was soba's formative stage. Soba noodles made with buckwheat flour alone have strong buckwheat flavor and are called *juwari*, meaning one-hundred percent. In contrast, soba noodles containing twenty-percent wheat flour are referred to as *ni-hachi*, or two-eight. Other popular varieties included Sarashina Soba and Yabu Soba. The former consists of flour milled from only the core of buckwheat seeds, resulting in white noodles and very elegant flavor, whereas the latter has a light green color which comes from milling the buckwheat seeds with the endocarp intact.

There were more than 3,500 soba restaurants in Edo (present-day Tokyo) by the latter half of the Edo period. Add to that the 3,000 soba stalls that are said to have existed in the city and you can start to imagine how much the people of Edo loved soba. The tradition for eating *toshikoshi* soba noodles on New Year's Eve also emerged during the Edo period. The long, thin noodles were considered an auspicious symbol of long life, and this tradition is still observed by many Japanese households. As with udon, many regional soba noodle dishes can be found around Japan. The three most famous are Nagano Prefecture's Togakushi Soba, Iwate Prefecture's Wanko Soba, and Izumo Soba from Shimane Prefecture.

Togakushi Soba

Wanko Soba

Izumo Soba

Homemade Udon Noodles

Not many Japanese people make udon noodles at home, but why not challenge yourself? Making them from scratch is actually not that difficult.

● Ingredients（serves 2）
  100 g cake flour
  100 g bread flour
  95-100 ml water
  10 g salt (just under 2 tsp)
  Extra bread flour, for kneading
  100 ml concentrated liquid soup base
  100 ml water
  Grated ginger and green onions, for garnish

● Directions

1 Add the salt to 95 ml of water and dissolve completely. Combine the two types of flour in a bowl, add the salt water and mix with long cooking chopsticks.

2 Once it starts coming together, use your hands to mix and make a ball of dough. If the dough feels dry and does not come together, add a little water (1 tsp). The dough should then loosely come together.

3 Knead the dough for five minutes until evenly kneaded then put in a plastic bag to rest for 30 minutes to 1 hour.

4 Remove dough from bag and knead for 1 minute. Return to plastic bag to rest for a further 15 minutes.

5 Sprinkle a thin layer of bread flour on a dry cutting board. Place the dough on the flour and use a rolling pin to roll to a thickness of 2-3 mm. Sprinkle the dough with plenty of flour and fold into three or four layers. Cut noodles to a width of 2-3 mm.

6 Sprinkle cut edges with flour to make sure the noodles do not stick to each other.

7 Fill a pot with plenty of water and bring to a boil. Place the udon noodles in the boiling water and stir. Cook for 7-8 minutes making sure the water does not boil over. Once cooked, transfer to iced water to cool. Drain water and serve noodles.

8 Dilute soup base with water to make dipping sauce and serve with grated ginger and chopped green onions.

TIPS The key with noodles is getting the water content right.
If you have trouble rolling out the dough, rest it a little longer.

Chapter 9 — Lunch Boxes - Bento and Ekiben

The earliest known form of Japanese lunch box, or bento, dates to the Heian period (794–1185) when cooked rice was sun-dried into a portable food called *hoshi-ii*. People placed the rice in water when they were ready to eat it. Travelers in the Edo period (1603–1868) carried rice balls wrapped in bamboo sheath, and

Makunouchi Bento

residents of Edo (present-day Tokyo) enjoyed lunch boxes at performances and during flower-viewing. One style still popular today is the Makunouchi Bento. With a name meaning "between acts," it was developed to be eaten during intermission.

Bento lunch boxes made by parents for small children and high school students have attracted a lot of attention in recent years. Japanese elementary and junior high schools provide hot school lunches, but this is not the case at most kindergartens or high schools, so parents (typically the mother) must make bento for their children. Bento are also required for special events at elementary school, such as sports carnivals and excursions, when hot lunches are not provided. Some parents invest a lot of time in creating *kyara-ben,* cute bento depicting cartoon characters.

Character bento come in many different forms. They often contain a small sausage shaped like an octopus, which can be made very easily by inserting cuts into one end of the sausage before frying in a pan. Shops sell specialized tools like seaweed cutters yielding shapes to turn simple *onigiri* rice balls into pandas. Opening a bento box to discover what is inside is such fun to a child's mind.

Octopus-shaped sausages

Kyara-ben character bento

While cute bento may delight a child, it can be a burden for parents especially if it becomes a competition. There is probably no other country in the world that expends this much energy on lunch boxes.

The actual boxes for Japanese bento come in a wide range of materials, shapes, and sizes. Especially cute ones are aimed at children, whereas adult bento boxes tend to be carefully designed and highly functional in terms of heat retention. Metal and plastic boxes are common, but a traditional wooden box made with a wood-bending technique called *magewappa* enhances the Japanese feel of lunchtime.

Ekiben are one of the essential joys of train travel. Literally meaning "station bento," *ekiben* refers to lunch boxes sold to travelers at stations or inside trains, including *shinkansen* bullet trains. More recently, the array of bento sold at airports have earned the name *soraben*, which can be translated as "sky bento."

Japanese railways underwent rapid development from the Meiji period (1868–1912) onwards prompting a rise in train travelers. The first-ever *ekiben* was apparently sold at Utsunomiya Station in 1885 and contained rice balls and pickled daikon. (Other theories exist.)

Luckily, eating bento in train carriages, along with drinking sake and beer, were not considered poor manners, and *ekiben* found its place as one of the pleasures of travel. Until the 1970s, in a scene familiar all over the country, salespeople carrying crates of bento walked the platforms selling through the windows of trains that had just arrived.

However, as high-speed trains became more common, carriage design changed such that windows no longer opened and stoppage times at stations shrunk, so nowadays it is extremely rare to see *ekiben* salespeople on platforms. Instead, travelers now purchase their bento at platform shops before boarding a train, or inside the train from the onboard sales wagon. Famous foods from places along the route are available from the wagon giving travelers a sense of the region even without calling into stations.

Japanese *ekiben* have seen incredible advancements since the first sales 150 years ago. There are currently

Onboard sales

2000–3000 different *ekiben* on sale at stations across Japan, and many seasonal *ekiben* made with fresh local ingredients are sold each year. While the average *ekiben* price is around 1000 yen, some premium varieties cost more than 3000 yen. One newer style relies on heat generated from the chemical reaction of mixing quicklime and water—a mechanism kicked off when a string on the bento is pulled.

There are some countries in the world where you can buy bento similar to *ekiben*, but none selling near as many varieties as seen in Japan. When next you find yourself traveling around Japan, rather than simply focusing on your destination, try an *ekiben* as one of the pleasures of the journey itself.

Self-heating bento

 *Onigiri* (Rice Balls)

Onigiri, made by shaping cooked rice in one's hands, come in four main styles. Triangular *onigiri* are found in Kanto and the rest of the country; those in Kansai are typically shaped like rice sacks; circular ones are often found in the Tohoku region; and spherical *onigiri* seen in central Japan are also referred to as *bakudan onigiri* or "rice bombs."

● Ingredients　(serves 3-4 (8 pieces))

800 g cooked rice
(approx. 360 g uncooked rice)
Small amount of salt
Toasted seaweed
<Fillings>
Okaka: 1 small packet of shaved bonito flakes
　　　　1/2 tsp soy sauce
Tsunamayo: 2 tbs canned tuna
　　　　　2 tsp mayonnaise
Shio-kombu: 1 tbs salted kombu strips
Ume-shiso: 1 *umeboshi* pickled plum
　　　　　1 tsp red *shiso furikake* seasoning powder

● Directions

1　Cook rice.

2　To make *okaka*, add soy sauce to bonito flakes and mix.

3　To make tuna mayo, drain oil from canned tuna, add mayonnaise and mix.

4　Moisten your hands with some water and sprinkle a pinch of salt on the palm of one hand. Scoop approximately 100 g of cooked rice onto the salted hand. Place the filling of your choice into the middle of the mound of rice and use both hands to shape as desired.

5　For *ume-shiso onigiri*, place 200 g of cooked rice in a bowl (makes 2). Add red *shiso furikake* and mix. Taking half of the prepared rice, follow step 4 but this time insert half of the *umeboshi* in the middle and shape each *onigiri* as desired.

6　Wrap *onigiri* with toasted seaweed.

TIPS　Other *onigiri* fillings include grilled salmon, salted cod roe (*tarako*), spicy cod roe (*mentaiko*), and salmon roe (*ikura*).

You can use plastic wrap when shaping *onigiri* to avoid rice sticking to your hands.

Wrapping prepared *onigiri* in plastic wrap makes them portable and avoids them drying out. To enjoy the crisp texture of toasted seaweed, wrap the seaweed just before eating.

Chapter 10 School Lunch

The Japanese word for lunch service is *kyushoku* and it typically refers to lunches provided at Japanese elementary and junior high schools. At present, almost every elementary school and 80% of junior high schools in Japan provide school lunch service. A fee of 200–300 yen per meal is collected from households and lunch  is prepared according to a monthly menu developed by school or municipal nutritionists. In principle, all students eat the same meal on a given day, and they cannot choose their food excepting cases of allergies or other health reasons(※1). Raw foods like sashimi and salads are not served for safety reasons. There are no cafeterias at schools that serve school lunch; students eat in their own classrooms. And it is customary for class teachers to eat the same meal in the classroom with their students. This is an integral component of their work as teachers because, in Japan, school lunch is treated as part of "Shokuiku" food and nutrition education.

School lunch service is said to have begun at a Yamagata Prefecture elementary school during the Meiji period (1868–1912). However, the style of *kyushoku* seen today was not established until the late 1940s in the post-World War II recovery period. Supplies of surplus wheat sent by the United States to relieve Japan's poor food situation were used to make school lunch. As a result, school lunch featured bread rather than rice, and sporks (spoon-fork hybrid utensils) in place of chopsticks.

Lunch served with a spork

   The post-war baby boom produced millions of children who grew up eating bread in school lunches—one reason for the subsequent Westernization of Japanese dietary habits. A domestic rice surplus in 1976 prompted the return of rice to school lunch. Modern school lunch menus show great diversity with Japanese, Western and Chinese variations in the regular monthly menu, and special thematic days featuring Japanese regional cuisine or dishes from countries around the world. Children get firsthand experience in food and nutrition education by tasting a wide range of dishes through *kyushoku*. Recently, deeper consideration of the "local production for local consumption" concept, encouraging proactive use of local ingredients, has spurred a movement for school lunch menus to incorporate local fish and vegetables as well as locally made miso and soy sauce.

Kyushoku is composed of fundamentally healthy foods, with menus built for nutritional balance. However, because children tend to prefer meat over fish and vegetables, cooks work really hard with different fish and vegetable preparation methods to create dishes that are both nutritious and delicious for children.

The following demonstrates the school lunch process for a junior high school with 850 students. The freshly cooked *kyushoku* is delivered every day from a nearby school lunch center, which is responsible for the school lunch of six local schools.

Specially trained cooks start at 7 a.m. every day to feed 4,800 students(※2). Once preparation is complete, they serve the lunch into vessels separated by school, year and class, and these are loaded into containers which are transported by truck to the schools around 11 a.m.

Staff unload the containers at the school and transport the year- and class-specific vessels to pantries on each floor. Around 12:30 p.m., at the end of fourth period, about five students on lunch duty from each class come wearing white apron coats to collect the *kyushoku* and take it to their classrooms.

Once the vessels are lined up across the front of the classroom, the remaining students line up with trays to receive the main dish, side dishes and milk before returning to their seats. The staple food on this particular day was bread because it was a Western-style meal.

When everyone has their food, a class representative stands at the front of the classroom to gratefully receive the food with the single word *itadakimasu* and everyone starts eating. The class teacher eats together with students in the classroom.

After eating, the representative stands again to say *gochisosama*, giving thanks for the meal, and one-by-one students return their dishes and utensils onto the racks they came on. These racks are designed to go directly into dishwashers, increasing efficiency for school lunch center staff. Each spoon has a hole in the handle which is passed onto a large metal loop for easy bundling. Students were making sure the spoons all faced the same way as they fed them onto the loop.

Kyushoku is about everyone eating the same meal; students are not free to choose only the foods they enjoy. It is possible to say, therefore, that the goal of Shokuiku is to give students opportunities to get acquainted with various dishes, ingredients and flavors to expand and develop their palates and reduce unbalanced diets.

Photo cooperation: Kanuma City Higashi Junior High School
Photo credit: Kazumi Hatasa

※1 : Students with known food allergies eat special lunches made without ingredients specified as allergens.

※2 : Some schools prepare the school lunch service at in-house kitchens.

Kare Raisu (Beef Curry with Rice)

A popular dish for school lunch, curry with rice is so loved by all from young to old that you could even describe it as a Japanese national dish. It is also often served at camps and retreats. Everyone has their own memories when it comes to curry.

● Ingredients （serves 4）

1 kg cooked rice (approx. 450 g uncooked rice)
200 g thinly sliced beef
1 carrot (150 g)
1 large onion (300 g)
2 small potatoes (200 g)
4 cups (800 ml) water
1 pack of curry cubes (to serve 4 people)
1 tbs oil
Pickled *rakkyo* scallions
Fukujinzuke pickled mixed vegetables

● Directions

1　Peel carrot and cut using the *rangiri* technique (starting from the tip, cut diagonally as you rotate the carrot 90 degrees between cuts). Cut onion into wedges. Peel potatoes and cut into 3 cm cubes. Cut beef into 4 cm strips.

2　Add oil to a pot and place over heat. Add beef and stir-fry just until the surface is browned. Add carrot, onion and potato and stir-fry for 2-3 minutes.

3　Add water and bring to a boil. Skim the froth from the surface then simmer on medium-low heat for 20 minutes.

4　Turn off heat, add curry cubes and dissolve. Turn on heat and simmer for additional 5 minutes.

5　Serve cooked rice into one side of a bowl and pour curry over.

6　Serve with *rakkyo* and *fukujinzuke* pickles.

TIPS　Store-brought curry base is typically sold in boxes of cubes, but also can be found in flake form.

Add garam masala, cumin and other spices as you please.

Other meats often found in curry include pork and chicken. It is not common to find Japanese curry made with lamb.

Adding eggplant, zucchini, paprika and other summer vegetables can add a seasonal touch to the curry.

Chapter 11

Regional Cuisine and B-Class Gourmet Cuisine

Kyodo-ryori refers to distinctive dishes of regional cuisine. They fit the locale, have been preserved over many generations, and use only ingredients that were available in the region before the development of food preservation technologies and transportation methods. From Hokkaido to Okinawa, countless regional dishes have been passed down since long ago. *Kyodo-ryori* exemplifies the concept of "local production for local consumption." That is because "the dishes are made with locally sourced seasonal ingredients and cooked according to traditional recipes developed locally" (from Kyodo-ryori Hyakusen(2007)).

In 2007, the Ministry of Agriculture, Forestry and Fisheries (MAFF) released a list of the top 100 regional Japanese foods based on the opinions of culinary researchers and food culture experts and an internet-based popular vote. MAFF identified 1,600 dishes from around Japan as candidates for the list, and the dish with the most popular votes was Yamagata Prefecture's *imo-ni* taro stew.

Imo-ni is specialty local cuisine from the Tohoku region of northern Japan made to time with the October taro harvest season. Locals began making the dish in the Edo period (1603–1868) and at first it contained only taro and other vegetables; no pork or beef as seen in modern versions. Even now in the regions of Tohoku besides Aomori Prefecture, it is common for families and friends to hold *Imo-ni Kai* events from October through November, gathering to cook and eat the stew together. They gather at the riverside on weekends, just like for picnics. There are some minor regional differences in Tohoku *imo-ni*. For example, in Yamagata Prefecture, it is made with beef and soy sauce in southern and central inland areas, but with pork and miso in seaside and all other areas. Versions in some other parts of Tohoku use chicken or fish. However, the common ingredient in all these variations is taro. (Note: potatoes are used in some areas along the Sanriku Coast spanning Aomori, Iwate and Miyagi prefectures.)

As the *Imo-ni Kai* season approaches, convenience

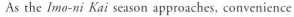

stores start selling firewood and supermarkets stock ingredient packs with everything needed for the stew. Scenes like this speak of autumn in Tohoku. *Imo-ni Kai* are very popular in Yamagata City, which is home to "Japan's No. 1 Imo-ni Kai Festival" held in September each year. Started in 1989, it is the largest

festival of its kind. Thirty-thousand servings of Yamagata-style *imo-ni* are made in six-meter-wide aluminum-alloy pans at the riverside venue with the help of heavy construction equipment.

Another category similar to *kyodo-ryori* regional cuisine is known in Japanese as "*B-kyu gotochi gurume.*" The term breaks down as follows: *gurume* is the Japanese notation for the French word "gourmet," *gotochi* means "local," and B *kyu* is a class lower than A showing that prices are not too high making the foods accessible for regular people. Essentially, the term means "B-class gourmet local cuisine" and is sometimes referred to as local soul food. In contrast with *kyodo-ryori,* the category includes dishes deeply intertwined with the region but created in the postwar period as well as relatively new dishes designed to revitalize a town or region. The inaugural B-1 Grand Prix nationwide contest in 2006 triggered the creation of a multitude of innovative dishes around Japan. Many tend to cater to the preferences of young people, including *yakisoba* stir-fried noodles, curries, and meat-based dishes. Some of the most well-known are Soup Curry from Sapporo, Hokkaido, Utsunomiya Gyoza from Tochigi Prefecture, and Fujinomiya Yakisoba from Shizuoka Prefecture.

Whether it is *kyodo-ryori* or *B-kyu gotochi gurume,* everyone loves to talk about food from their hometown. It is a great conversation starter when talking with Japanese people and a helpful reference when choosing restaurants. And knowing about some regional foods before traveling to new parts of Japan always adds some fun to your adventures.

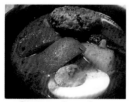

Sapporo Soup Curry

Utsunomiya Gyoza

Fujinomiya Yakisoba

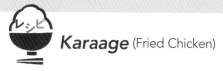

Karaage (Fried Chicken)

An incredibly popular dish in lunch boxes and as a snack with a cold beer. Delicious as a cold dish, but nothing compares to just-fried *karaage* with its crisp outside and juicy middle. Every family has their own recipe using different seasonings such as soy sauce, salt, ginger and garlic.

● Ingredients (serves 2-3)

300 g chicken thigh meat
A │ 1 tbs sake
　│ 1 tsp soy sauce
　│ 1/3 tsp (2 g) salt
1 tsp ginger juice (or grated ginger)
1 tbs wheat flour
Vegetable oil
Lemon, for garnish

● Directions

1　Cut chicken thigh meat into 4-5 cm cubes.

2　Combine chicken, ingredients in A and ginger juice and allow to marinate for at least 10 minutes.

3　Sprinkle chicken from step 2 with flour. Fry in 160-170°C shallow oil for 3-4 minutes then remove from pan. Raise oil temperature to 180°C, return chicken and fry a second time for about 2 minutes until cooked through.

4　Serve with lemon wedges, if desired.

 TIPS　Marinate chicken overnight in the refrigerator to soak up more flavor and tenderize the chicken.

Mixing a small amount of egg white with the chicken and increasing the amount of flour in the coating results in thicker, crunchier batter. Potato starch can be substituted for wheat flour.

Using store-bought tubes of grated garlic and ginger simplifies the preparation process. Experiment with the seasoning to find your favorite combination.

Chapter 12

Food Culture and Values

Many foreign tourists to Japan say their visit is motivated by the desire to enjoy Japanese food. The number of foreigners and their families living in Japan for study or work is increasing every year, giving rise to multiple coexisting food cultures—a situation which then impacts Japanese food culture. In this book we introduced the history of limitations in Japanese diets, and we will consider here how that made Japanese people aware of their own values and led to tolerance for other people's values around food.

Animals, be they herbivores or carnivores, must eat in order to survive. They eat when hungry choosing suitable foods by instinct without constraints. Humans, as animals, are no exception. However, the highly developed intellect of humans led to the establishment of limits and principles not based on instinct but on religion, ethics and values. Those concepts have been implemented as food taboos.

Food taboos exist all over the world and the most typical are those based on religion. In Judaism, dietary laws known as *kashruth* specify the types of animals suitable for consumption and acceptable slaughter methods. Adherents of Islam do not eat pork as pigs are considered unclean. And in Hinduism, cows are thought to be sacred messengers for the gods and thus not to be consumed.

In Japan, too, certain food restrictions existed in the past. Buddhism, which forbids the killing of living things, was introduced to Japan from the Asian continent in the mid-6th century. In the 13th century, Zen monk training included the challenge of making ever more delicious meals without fish and meat. Limited to plant-based foods like vegetables and beans, a series of innovations gave birth to vegetarian Buddhist cuisine called *shojin ryori*.

A seventh-century emperor issued an order to commoners forbidding specific forms of hunting and fishing as well as the consumption of meat from cattle, horses, dogs, monkeys, and chickens. Japan was an agrarian society focused on rice production, so it was not rational to eat cattle, horses and other work animals raised to plough fields and rice paddies. Concerned about poor harvests caused by bad weather and natural disasters, emperors from the eighth century onwards issued directives forbidding the taking of life and consumption of meat as a vow to the gods. Thus, for approximately 1,200 years from the late seventh century until the Edo period (1603–1868) the Japanese hardly ever openly ate meat, and meals consisted of soybean-based foods, fish and vegetables. They did, however, eat wild animals such as pheasant, wild boar and deer. Some people even disguised their consumption of meat with the euphemism *kusurigui*, alluding to it as medicinal food.

Japanese eating habits changed drastically after the Meiji Restoration in 1868. This is because the government encouraged the consumption of animal flesh out of fear for the diminutive Japanese physique compared to Westerners. Some Japanese initially resisted the change finding consumption of meat unclean, but beef and pork gradually entered the diet.

Buta no kakuni
(braised pork belly)

Shojin ryori had a major influence on cooking methods found in Japanese cuisine. Restaurants of this Buddhist cuisine can be found near temples, but it is also interesting to experience temple life and eat *shojin ryori* through an overnight temple stay called *shukubo*. Some dishes called *modoki ryori* imitate meat dishes with *fu* wheat gluten or soybean products. One dish known as

Shojin ryori

ganmodoki, a deep-fried dumpling of vegetables mixed through tofu, was named for its resemblance to the meat of *gan* wild geese.

One Japanese food that provokes international debate is whale. Eating whale meat has been a Japanese custom since around the 12th century. In the beginning, people ate the meat of whales that washed up on the shore, considering them a blessing from the sea. Active fishing of whales only began after that. In the 19th century,

Whale bacon

England and America hunted whales to use their oil as machine lubricant, but they did not eat the flesh. Whaling countries including Japan have continued research whaling from the standpoint of preventing resource depletion, but countries opposed to whaling say the very catching of whales should be prohibited, and little progress has been made toward mutual understanding.

The documentary film *The Cove* (※1) shone a spotlight on dolphin drive hunting in the town of Taiji in Wakayama Prefecture. That the dolphins are hunted for consumption does not seem to make it any more acceptable in some other countries' cultures(※2). For the local people, however, it is a tradition from long ago and they express a desire not to be judged according to the values of other cultures.

The judgment of whether certain foods can or must not be eaten is governed by ethics and values that were formulated by humans and can therefore said to be arbitrary. Thus, evaluating another country's food culture poses difficult questions even when the importance of mutual respect for each other's values is understood.

※1 : US documentary film released in 2009.
※2 :In 2018, a film called *Okujirasama—Futatsu no Seigi no Monogatari* (A Whale of a Tale) was made giving a balanced perspective of pro- and anti-whaling standpoints.

 **Nikujaga** (Meat and Potatoes)

When you ask people in Japan to name the dish that "reminds them of home," many name a meat and potato dish called *nikujaga*. The choice of meat and seasoning differs by region and even household, and here we introduce a slightly sweet version with plenty of sauce.

● Ingredients (serves 3-4)

200 g thinly sliced beef
2 large potatoes (approx. 400 g)
1 medium onion (approx. 200 g)
1 small carrot (approx. 100 g)
5-6 beans (approx. 30 g)
2 tbs oil
600 ml dashi
  3 cups (600 ml) water
  1 tsp powdered Japanese soup stock
2 tbs soy sauce
4 tbs sugar

● Directions

1   Peel potatoes and cut into eighths. Place in a bowl of water.

2   Peel carrot and cut using the *rangiri* technique (starting from the tip, cut diagonally as you rotate the carrot 90 degrees between cuts). Cut onion into wedges.

3   Place a large pot over heat and coat the surface with oil. Add beef and stir-fry just until the surface is browned. Add carrot, onion and potato and stir-fry for additional 2-3 minutes.

4   Add the dashi liquid and bring to a boil over medium-high heat. Skim the froth from the surface.

5   Cut a piece of parchment paper into a circle that fits just inside the pot. Rest it on top of the ingredients and simmer on medium-low heat for 10 minutes.

6   Add the sugar and 1 tbs of soy sauce. Simmer for approximately 10 more minutes until potatoes are tender.

7   Cut beans into bite-size pieces. In a separate pot, boil the beans in lightly salted water for 1-2 minutes and transfer immediately to iced water to cool.

8   Add the beans and the remaining 1 tbs of soy sauce to the pot and stir briefly.

TIPS   Pork also works well. In Kanto, this recipe typically contains pork, whereas in Kansai it usually contains beef.

For richer flavor, add more sugar and soy sauce. As long as they are added in equal amounts, the dish should not become too sweet.

This recipe leaves some of the liquid as sauce, but it is also possible to simmer the dish until all the liquid has been absorbed.

Chapter **13** Ramen

Ramen is a favorite dish of many, as well-known around the world as sushi. Japanese ramen is typically composed of Chinese noodles in soup finished with vegetables, roast pork slices, egg and other toppings. There is no question that it developed from a Chinese noodle dish called *lamian*, but the two are not synonymous to the Chinese, who distinguish them by calling the Japanese noodle dish "Japanese-style *lamian*." Ramen can be enjoyed at specialty ramen shops, but is also extremely popular in instant ramen and cup noodle varieties that people prepare themselves.

Shoyu ramen
(ramen in
soy sauce-based soup)

The yellow noodles found in ramen are called *chukamen* in Japanese, meaning "Chinese noodles." They are made from wheat, salt, and an alkaline liquid called *kansui,* or lye water, originally from Mongolia. Flavonoid pigments in the wheat react to the alkalinity and turn yellow to create the distinctive color and aroma

Chinese noodles

of ramen noodles. It should be noted that there are many Chinese noodles that do not include this liquid.

There are approximately 26,500 ramen shops in Japan (2020 survey, iTownPage, https://itp.ne.jp/). Ramen's history began in the Meiji period (1868–1912) with records showing a dish called Nanking Soba served at the Yowaken eatery in Hokkaido as Japan's first ramen. Opened in 1910, Rairaiken in Asakusa was the first specialty ramen shop in Tokyo. The dish grew popular around Japan thereafter, but it was not yet known as ramen; it was called *shina soba* or *chuka soba* to indicate its Chinese origins and distinguish it from Japanese soba noodles.

The Chinese word *lamian* means "pulled noodles," but the name is not entirely accurate because Japanese ramen is not hand-pulled but made by cutting dough, just like udon and soba. The most dominant theory on the origin of the name ramen comes from Sapporo's Takeya Shokudo. The eatery opened in 1921 in Sapporo City, Hokkaido, right near Hokkaido University. It began as a regular eatery but was reborn as Chinese Food Takeya in 1922 with the arrival of a Chinese chef. The eatery thrived, supported by the presence of Chinese exchange students at Hokkaido University. One favorite menu item was *shina soba* served in salt-based soup. But finding the term *shina soba* derogatory, the owner's wife set about making a new name. The one she came up with linked the sound "ra" in the chef's loud call declaring the dish ready to serve with "men" meaning noodles, to make the word ramen.

Chinese restaurants spread at a steady pace in the early 20th century until they were dealt a catastrophic blow with the 1923 Great Kanto Earthquake. Restaurant chefs served ramen at stalls to aid recovery from the disaster and some opened businesses outside of Tokyo, contributing to the spread of ramen nationwide. There has again been a continuous rise in the number of ramen shops since the end of World War II.

Ramen stall

In 1958, ramen became a household name across Japan with the launch of the first-ever instant version—Nissin Chicken Ramen—made simply by adding boiling water and waiting three minutes. Nissin Foods then released instant ramen in a cup in 1971, and these "cup noodles" saw explosive sales because they were so convenient and delicious. Sales even overtook those of packet instant noodles in 1989. Cup noodles became available in countries all over the world spawning many new flavors including Southeast Asian varieties like Tom Yum Kung hot and sour soup.

Instant ramen   Cup noodles

In Japan you can find ramen-themed entertainment venues like the Shin-Yokohama Ramen Museum. Visitors to these so-called thematic restaurants can taste ramen from popular stores around Japan all in one place. And in big Japanese cities, you can often find places like Sapporo Ramen Yokocho with a concentration of ramen shops in one alley. In the past, the choices were limited to soy sauce, salt or miso-based soups, but the variations now seem endless, including pork bone broth (*tonkotsu*), chicken bone broth (*torigara*) and seafood-based soup (*gyokai*) made with bonito and sardines. Shops specialize in noodles ranging from thick to thin and straight or curly, and customers can sometimes even specify the cook time to get the noodles to their preferred firmness.

Sapporo Ramen Yokocho

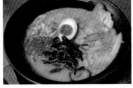

Thick noodles/ thin noodles

Miso ramen

Tonkotsu ramen

Recent popular styles include *tsukemen*—noodles dipped in soup instead of served inside it—and *abura soba* in which the diner tosses the noodles in an oil-sauce mixture. Originating in China but adapted in Japan, Japanese ramen is no longer recognized as a Chinese dish even among the Chinese. It is fun to try many styles and find your favorite bowl.

Tsukemen

Abura soba

Ramen Noodles with *Nitamago* Seasoned Boiled Egg

Nitamago seasoned boiled eggs are a favorite ramen topping and they are really easy to make at home. The flavor of the half-boiled egg with a thick, yolky center changes based on the amount of time spent in the soy sauce-based marinating liquid.

Seasoned boiled eggs

● Ingredients

5-6 eggs

A | 3 tbs soy sauce
  | 2 tbs sake (or white wine)
  | 1 tbs sugar

● Directions

1 Fill a pot with water and bring to a boil. Gently place eggs in the pot and boil for 8 minutes.

2 Remove the eggs from the pot and transfer immediately to cold water. Remove shells and place eggs in a sealable plastic bag with the ingredients in A. Seal bag making sure to remove as much air as possible.

3 Place marinating eggs in a refrigerator for 6 hours. Eggs are then ready to eat or can be stored in a refrigerator for 2-3 days.

Ramen noodles

● Ingredients（serves 1）

300 ml hot water

A | 1 tsp chicken stock powder
  | 1 tbs soy sauce
  | a pinch of pepper

1 seasoned boiled egg

Green onions, *naruto* fish cake with a whirlpool pattern, and *menma* fermented bamboo shoots, for topping.

● Directions

1 Heat water in a pan and add ingredients in A to make the ramen soup. (You can also add hot water to soup packets that come with the noodles.) Cut green onions, *naruto*, *menma* and any other toppings of choice.

2 In a separate pot, boil water and cook the noodles (follow instructions on package).

3 To a deep serving bowl, add the hot soup from step 1 and the drained noodles from step 2. Cut seasoned boiled egg in half and place on top with other toppings.

TIPS   The most important thing when making seasoned boiled eggs is to correctly measure the boiling time. After 7 1/2 minutes the yolk will still be quite runny, but by 8 1/2 minutes it will be firm.

When left to marinate for a long time, seasoned boiled eggs become very salty. Try increasing the amount of sake to 3 tbs for longer marinating times.

Eel is typically enjoyed as *unagi no kabayaki*—eel dipped in salty-sweet seasoning and broiled. Along with sushi, tempura and soba, *unagi no kabayaki* is one of the top four Edo dishes created during the Edo period (1603–1868). With approximately 2,800 eel restaurants nationwide (Town Page Database 2011), eel can be enjoyed anywhere in Japan. Until around 2000, Japan

Unaju broiled eel served over rice in a box

consumed about 70% of the world's eel production, but a Japanese food boom has caused large increases in consumption outside Japan, in China and other countries of Asia.

The Japanese have been eating eel for over 1,000 years, but it was not until the *kabayaki* method was created in the Edo period that it gained the level of popularity seen today. To make the dish, eel is put on skewers, dipped in a mixture of soy sauce, mirin and sugar, and cooked directly over charcoals. The smell of charring soy sauce is so appetizing that one *rakugo* traditional comic tale depicts a miserly man who makes only his rice before proceeding to dine on the aromas wafting up from the eel shop below.

The flavor combination yielded by soy sauce, mirin and sugar is called *amakara*. It is the same salty-sweet flavor found in sukiyaki, *gyudon* beef bowls, and teriyaki chicken. Two important developments in the Edo period gave birth to the *amakara* flavor: the advent of local sugar production in Japan, and later, the start of mass production of *koikuchi shoyu* dark-colored soy sauce in the towns of Noda and Choshi in Chiba Prefecture. The seasoning sauce helped hide the muddy smell often found in river fish like *unagi*, and was a great match for its flesh, spurring widespread popularity for *unagi no kabayaki*.

A likely theory for the origin of the term *kabayaki* is in

Eel

Kabayaki

Bulrush plant head

a 15th century cooking method in which eels were cut into portions but not gutted before being skewered for broiling. Their resemblance to the heads of bulrush plants, or *gama*, led to the dish name *gamayaki* whose pronunciation subsequently morphed into *kabayaki*. Even though the current preparation involves skewering cleaned, filleted pieces of eel, the Japanese character for *gama* is still used but with the reading *kabayaki*.

It is custom in Japan to eat *unagi* on a certain day at the end of July. Called "Doyo no Ushi no Hi," it falls on a different day each year somewhere in the second half of the month. When July comes around, many people wonder what day it will be and get excited about eating *unagi no kabayaki*. But in actual fact, *unagi* can be enjoyed year-round and the best season is winter. Despite this, the month with the highest consumption in Japan is always July. The charts below show monthly and daily (July-only) figures for expenditure on *unagi no kabayaki* in 2002. They clearly demonstrate the overwhelming increase in expenditure around July 20—the "Doyo no Ushi no Hi" that year.

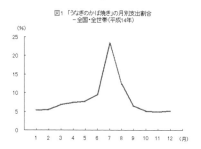

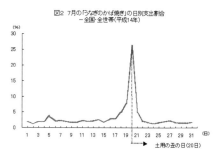

http://www.stat.go.jp/data/kakei/topics/topics04.htm
(Statistics Bureau, Ministry of Internal Affairs and Communications, 2002)

There are various stories for the Japanese custom of eating *unagi* on this day, but the most compelling account is as follows. An *unagi* store suffering from poor sales in the summer period consulted an academic called Hiraga Gennai. He suggested a marketing strategy promoting *unagi* as a midsummer food to prevent heat exhaustion. The campaign was a huge success, thereby establishing the tradition of eating *unagi* in the heat of summer.

Records show, however, that awareness of eel as a highly nutritious food existed well before that time. Two poems about eels by the poet Otomo no Yakamochi can be found in the 8th century text *Manyoshu* (literally "Collection of Ten Thousand Leaves").

石麻呂に　吾物申す　夏痩せに　良しといふ物ぞ　鰻漁り食せ

Ishimaro ni   waremono mosu   natsu yase ni   yoshi to ifu mono zo   munagi tori mese
(To Iwamaro I say this: If you've slimmed down in summer. There's one thing that works: Catch and eat eels!)

痩す痩すも　生けらばあらむを　はたやはた　鰻を漁ると　川に流るな

Yasu yasu mo   ikeraba aramu o   hata yahata   munagi o toru to   kawa ni nagaru na
(If you keep on thinning. To keep on living, Here's what you should do: Catch eels, but Don't fall in the river!)

Otomo no Yakamochi composed these *waka* traditional poems for his friend Yoshida Ishimaro, seemingly a very skinny man. The first poem implores him to go and catch eels to gain some vitality. In the second one the poet taunts his friend saying even if you are skinny you have to stay alive, but make sure not to fall in the river when you go eel-catching. The two appear to have been great friends. Perhaps Hiraga Gennai—the Edo period mind behind eating eel on "Doyo no Ushi no Hi"—was aware of these poems when he came up with his strategy to boost sales.

Ninety-nine percent of all *unagi* consumed in Japan is farmed. Glass eels (elvers) about five centimeters in length are caught in nets to be raised in aquaculture for one-and-a-half years. Dramatic declines in glass eel catches in recent years have highlighted the need for greater efforts to secure this natural resource.

 *Oyako-don* (Chicken and Egg Bowl)

The name of this popular rice bowl dish refers to "parent and child" (*oyako*), with the parent being the chicken, and the egg the child. The topping is simmered in a sweet soy sauce blend. Adjust the amount of sugar and soy sauce to your taste.

 Ingredients (serves 2-3)

160 g chicken (thigh meat)
1/2 large onion (approx. 150 g)
3 eggs
1/2 bunch of *mitsuba* trefoil
Dashi 250 ml water
   1/4 tsp powdered Japanese soup stock
2 tbs sugar
1 tbs soy sauce
Shichimi seven spice mix or *kona-zansho* ground Japanese pepper, if desired

● Directions

1 Peel onion, cut in half, then cut into 5 mm-wide strips. Cut chicken into 2 cm cubes. Cut *mitsuba* into 3 cm-lengths.

2 Crack the eggs into a bowl and beat lightly.

3 Put dashi, sugar and soy sauce in a pan. Place over medium-high heat to bring to a boil. Once boiled, add onion and cook for 2-3 minutes.

4 Add chicken and cook for 2-3 minutes. Once the chicken is cooked, add the lightly beaten egg in a long steady stream distributed evenly around the pot. Lastly, add *mitsuba*.

5 Put the lid on the pan for 20 seconds then turn off heat. Allow the excess heat to partially cook the egg.

6 Fill a deep bowl with cooked rice. Top with the ingredients and sauce from step 5.

7 Sprinkle with *shichimi* or *kona-zansho*, if desired.

TIPS   If you prefer the egg well-done, extend the cooking time in step 5.

Mitsuba is a herb with a unique aroma. If not available, it can be substituted with parsley or other herbs.

Chapter 15 Okonomiyaki

Grains milled into powder form are part of the food culture in many countries around the world. In Japan, flour-based dishes are referred to as *konamono* (or *konamon)* and include foods such as udon, soba, ramen, wontons, pasta, pizza, tortillas and Korean-style savory pancakes, as well as sweet varieties like cakes, doughnuts,

Kansai-style *okonomiyaki*

pancakes and crepes. In this book we highlight three of the most popular Japanese *konamono* dishes: *okonomiyaki, takoyaki* and *monjayaki.*

Okonomiyaki Savory Pancakes:

The origin of *okonomiyaki* is said to be in a 16th century tea ceremony sweet called *funoyaki* first made by tea ceremony master Sen no Rikyu, but the prototype for modern *okonomiyaki* was a dish sold at a Tokyo stall in the 1930s (※1). The dish was introduced to Osaka and spread from there until interrupted by World War II. It was revived in the post-war recovery period and a rich, viscous sauce replaced the traditional Worcestershire sauce topping, giving birth to the dish now called Kansai-style *okonomiyaki.* Also known as *mazeyaki* (mixed to cook), ingredients like shredded cabbage, meat, shrimp, and squid are mixed through a wheat flour–based batter before being cooked on a *teppan* hot plate like a pancake. Grated Japanese yam (*yamaimo*) is sometimes included in the batter for lighter, fluffier texture. The mixture is flipped to cook on both sides and topped with the special thick sauce, bonito flakes, powdered green laver, and mayonnaise just before eating. The freedom to choose ingredients within as well as toppings gave the dish its name, which translates as "cooked as you like it." At some *okonomiyaki* restaurants, a hot plate is installed at each table and diners cook their own foods.

Hiroshima-style *okonomiyaki* got its start when many *okonomiyaki* stalls appeared in Hiroshima after war reduced the city to burnt fields. It emerged as a local dish in a time when food shortages complicated the gathering of ingredients. Hiroshima-style *okonomiyaki* is differentiated by its method in which ingredients are placed on top of each other (*noseyaki* ※2) rather than mixed together. A thin layer of wheat flour–based batter is first spread like a crepe to cook on the hot plate. A mound of shredded cabbage about 15 centimeters high is piled on the crepe, followed by layers of pork, shrimp, squid and other ingredients. The whole pile is then flipped to steam-cook the cabbage, after which egg and other ingredients may be added. Once brushed with *okonomi* sauce and topped with powdered green laver, chopped green onions, and mayonnaise, it is ready to serve. Diners never cook their own food at Hiroshima-style *okonomiyaki* eateries.

Hiroshima-style *okonomiyaki*

Takoyaki Grilled Octopus Dumplings

This dish was invented in Osaka in the 1930s. It is a Kansai soul food indicative of the tastes of ordinary people in the region. A batter made from wheat flour dissolved in water or dashi is poured to overflowing into hemi-spherical molds. Cooks add a piece of octopus to each and then use metal skewers to turn repeatedly and shape the batter into balls. Once topped with a

Takoyaki

special sauce, bonito flakes, and powdered green laver, they are ready to eat—crisp on the outside and hot and gooey in the middle. Diners stab the dumplings with toothpicks or bamboo skewers to pick them up and eat. By the 1960s, *takoyaki* stands could also be found in the Kanto region from where they spread nationwide to become a staple at festivals and other events. Chain stores making *takoyaki* for takeout appeared in the 1990s and *takoyaki* shops can now be found in almost every corner of the country. Nowadays, commercial *takoyaki* pans make it easy for households to make their own and *takoyaki* parties are popular among children and young adults.

Takoyaki stand

Takoyaki machine

Monjayaki Thin Seasoned Savory Pancake:

Monjayaki was created in Edo (present-day Tokyo) in the first decade of the 1800s. Made on a hot plate, it was originally a dish called *mojiyaki* or "cooked characters." Children would write characters with a batter of flour and water and eat the cooked result, as seen in an 1819 picture in *Hokusai Manga* by famous ukiyo-e artist Katsushika Hokusai. *Mojiyaki* became popular from the late Edo period (1603–1868) through the Meiji period (1868–1912) as a food children could make themselves in a corner of their local *dagashiya* mom-and-pop candy store. Somewhere along the way the name transformed from *mojiyaki* to *monjayaki*. Compared to *okonomiyaki,* the ratio of water to flour is higher in *monjayaki* and seasonings like soy sauce and other sauces are mixed through the batter before cooking. Typical ingredients include cabbage, meat and seafood, but it is also common to add spicy cod roe, mochi and cheese. Generally speaking, diners cook the dish themselves. Chatting and catching up while using small individual spatulas called *kote* to press and cook the batter on the hot plate is all part of the fun of eating *monjayaki.*

Monjayaki

Kote

※1   Old-fashioned *okonomiyaki* store Furyu Okonomiyaki Sometaro opened in 1938 and still operates in Asakusa today in a highly atmospheric old-style Japanese home.

※2   Also called *kasaneyaki,* meaning "layered to cook."

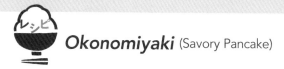

Okonomiyaki (Savory Pancake)

All you need to make *okonomiyaki* pancakes are *okonomiyaki* sauce, cabbage, flour and eggs. Add different toppings to create your own original recipe.

● Ingredients（serves 2-3）

<Batter>
50 g cake flour (5 rounded tablespoons)
60 ml water
1/2 tsp powdered Japanese soup stock
1 egg
3 tbs (approx. 10 g) *tenkasu* tempura batter crumbs
1-2 tbs grated *yamaimo* Japanese yam
1 tsp oil

<Fillings>
5-6 thin slices of pork (50 g)
2-3 cabbage leaves (100 g)
✳ seafood, beef, *yakisoba* noodles, cheese, kimchi,
spicy cod roe (mentaiko), mochi,
red pickled ginger (*beni-shoga*), green onions etc.

<Sauce and Toppings>
2 tbs *okonomiyaki* sauce
1 tsp bonito flakes
1/2 tsp *aonori* dried green seaweed
Mayonnaise, if desired

● Directions

1　In a large bowl mix water, powdered soup stock and flour to make the batter.

2　Chop cabbage leaves into strips approximately 3-4 mm wide.

3　Add cabbage, egg, *tenkasu* and grated *yamaimo* to batter from step 1.

4　Heat a frying pan and add the oil. Arrange the pork slices then pour the batter from step 3 over the top, spreading it into a circle about 1.5–2 cm thick.

5　Place lid on pan and cook on medium-low heat for 4-5 minutes. Flip over and cook further for 3-4 minutes.

6　Top with *okonomiyaki* sauce and sprinkle with bonito flakes and *aonori*. Top with mayonnaise, if desired.

TIPS　Make sure to peel the *yamaimo* before grating. This recipe can be made without the *yamaimo* if not available.

If *okonomiyaki* sauce is not available, can be substituted with *tonkatsu* sauce or *chuno* sauce.

Store-bought *okonomiyaki* powder can be used instead of flour for the batter. Follow instructions on package.

料理のことば

切り方

○○cm角	縦横の長さと高さを○○ cm で同じ立方体に切ること。 Cut into cubes with equal length, width and height of ○○cm.	
いちょう切り	イチョウの葉のように円の 1/4 の形に切ること。 Cut into quarter-circle slices like the shape of a ginkgo leaf.	
くし形に切る くし形切り	トマトやレモンなど、丸い形のものを放射状に切ること。日本のくしの形に似せた切り方。 Cut round ingredients such as tomatoes and lemons into wedges. The resulting shape resembles a Japanese comb.	
小口切り	ねぎやごぼうなど細くて丸くて長いものを細かく切ること。 Finely chop long, thin, round vegetables such as green onions and burdock root.	
さいの目切り	サイコロのように正方形で縦横の高さ、長さが同じ立方体に切ること。 Cut into cubes like dice, with equal length, width and height.	
ささがき	ごぼうなどを、細く長く削るように切ること。 Cut burdock root into long, thin shavings.	
せん切り	1～3mm 幅に細長く切ること。「千切り」とも書く。 Cut into long, thin strips approximately 1-3 mm wide. Also written as 千切り.	
短冊切り	人参などを、縦横比 3：1 程度の長方形に薄く切ること。短冊とは短歌や俳句を書くための長方形の紙で、その形に似せた切り方。 Cut carrot and other vegetables into rectangular slices with a height to width ratio of approximately 3:1. The cutting style is named for its resemblance to *tanzaku*—rectangular strips of paper traditional Japanese poems are written on.	
半月切り	半月に似せて円を 1/2 の形に切ること。「半月切り / 半月に切る」という。 Cut into half-circle slices like a half moon.	
乱切り	人参などの棒状、またはじゃがいもなどの円形のものを、形は違っても同じくらいの大きさにそろえて多面的に切ること。 Cut different-shaped vegetables such as carrots and potatoes into similar sizes with multiple surfaces.	

アクを取る すくう	肉類、魚介類、野菜類などに含まれる雑味成分をアクと呼ぶ。煮立てるとアクが泡のように浮いてくるので、それを取って捨てること。 *Aku* refers to components in meat, seafood and vegetables that add unfavorable flavor to a dish. When a liquid containing such ingredients comes to a boil, *aku* forms a foam on the surface. This should be removed and discarded.
油ぬき	油揚げや厚揚げに熱湯をかけて油を流して除くこと。 To pour boiling water on deep-fried tofu (*abura-age* and *atsu-age*) to remove excess oil.
色止め	緑色野菜をゆでた後、野菜の色が悪くならないように冷水に浸すこと。 To immerse cooked green vegetables in cold water to preserve color.
かため	少しかたい状態。少しやわらかい状態は「やわらかめ」。 Slightly firm. Slightly soft is referred to as *yawarakame*.
紙蓋	和紙やクッキングペーパーなどの紙を鍋の落とし蓋用に切ったもの。煮る時に材料にかぶせる。 *Washi* Japanese paper or paper towel cut to make a lid for a pot, which is placed on top of ingredients during simmering.
からりと	天ぷらやとんかつなどの揚物を揚げた時の仕上がりの良い状態。衣がサクッと軽い食感で、油っぽくない。 Description of perfectly cooked deep-fried foods like tempura and *tonkatsu* breaded pork cutlet. The coating is crisp and light, not oily.
切り込み 切れ目を入れる	材料に浅く包丁を入れて切ること。 To insert shallow cuts into ingredients.
こす	こし器やキッチンペーパーなどに材料を通して、液体と固体を分けたり、カスなどを取り除いて均一の状態にすること。 To pass ingredients through a sieve or paper towel to separate liquid and solid components or to remove unnecessary pieces for a smooth consistency.
こんがり きつね色	フライパンやオーブンなどで焼くときの焼き色や、油で揚げるときの揚げ色が、おいしそうに茶色く色づいた状態。焦げる前段階の色。 The appetizing brown color of foods cooked in a frying pan or oven, or deep-fried in oil. It describes the color achieved in the stage before burning.
塩ひとつまみ	親指・ひとさし指・中指の三本の指先でつまむ量。約1g相当。 An amount that can be pinched between the thumb, and pointer and index fingers. Approximately 1 g.
しっとりする	水分を含んでやわらかく湿った状態。 A tender, juicy and moist state.
ちぎる	手でひっぱったり、つまんだりして切り分けること。 To cut into pieces by pulling or breaking off with one's hands.

つけあわせ	肉料理や魚料理の横に添える野菜や副菜のこと。英語の garnish、side dish など。 Vegetables and other sides served with meat or seafood dishes. Often referred to in English as a garnish or side dish.
（卵を）溶く	卵黄と卵白をかき混ぜて均一にすること。塩や砂糖を水に混ぜて均一にすることは「溶かす」という。 To mix egg yolk and white until combined. Dissolving salt or sugar in water is described as *tokasu*.
二度揚げ	低温の油（160-170℃）で揚げた後、一度取り出して、再び高温の油（180℃）で揚げ色をつけて揚げる方法。厚みのある肉でも中まで火を通して上手に揚げることができる。 Frying method with two steps: first fry at low temperature (160-170℃) and remove, then fry again at a high temperature (180℃) for golden color. This method makes it possible to nicely cook even thick pieces of meat through to the middle.
寝かせる	生地や合わせた材料・調味料をしばらく置いておくこと。詳しくはp79 参照。 To allow dough, combined ingredients, or combined seasonings to rest for a time. Refer to page 79 for details.
パサつく	水分が少なく少し乾燥した状態。本来、乾燥しない方がよいものが乾燥している時に使うネガティブな表現。 When something dries out because of low moisture content. It is a negative expression used when something that should not be dry has dried out.
ふきこぼれ	火が強すぎて、鍋の中の茹で水や煮汁が鍋の外に出てしまうこと。 When the heat is too high causing water or simmering liquid in a pot to boil over.
分量外	レシピの材料表に入っていないもの。 Ingredients not included in the recipe's ingredients list.
ほぐす	卵黄と卵白をくずして軽く混ぜること。 To break the egg yolk and white and mix lightly.
まぶす	食材のまわりに小麦粉やパン粉などの粉や、タレなどの液体を均一につけること。「まぶしつける」ともいう。 To evenly coat ingredients with powders or liquids such as flour, breadcrumbs or sauce. Also described as *mabushitsukeru*.
まわし入れる	液体などを鍋に入れるときに細く垂らしながら、全体にまわしながら入れること。 To make a long, steady stream that is distributed evenly when adding liquids to a pot.
水でもどす	乾物（干しシイタケや乾燥わかめなど）を、水に長時間入れてやわらかくすること。 To soften dehydrated ingredients (dried shiitake and wakame) by soaking in water for an extended period.

湯をきる （ゆ）	麺や野菜をゆでた後、ザルにあげて振りながら湯を捨てること。 To discard boiling water after cooking noodles and vegetables by transferring them to a colander and shaking.
よそう	ごはんや汁物をお椀に入れる時に、適度な量で美しく盛り付けること。 To nicely present an appropriate amount of food when serving rice and soups into bowls.
余熱 （よねつ）	加熱した後の食材、鍋やフライパンが保持している熱のこと。火を止めた後もこの余熱によって加熱が継続する。 The heat retained by ingredients, pots or frying pans after heating. Heating continues even after turning off the heat source because of this residual heat.
割り入れる （わ　い）	卵の殻を割って、ボウルなどに卵の中身を入れること。 To crack the contents of an egg into a bowl.

参考文献

第1章／Chapter1

北岡正三郎　『物語　食の文化―美味い話、味な知識』　中央新書　2011

原田信男　『日本人はなにを食べてきたか』角川ソフィア文庫　2010

「日本料理（Japanese culinary art and culture）の 世界無形文化遺産登録に向けた提案書」　農林水産省
　　https://www.maff.go.jp/j/keikaku/syokubunka/meeting/4/pdf/4than02_kyoto.pdf（1/1/2021 閲覧）

「ユネスコ無形文化遺産　和食」　農林水産省
　　https://www.maff.go.jp/j/keikaku/syokubunka/ich/（1/1/2021 閲覧）

第2章／Chapter2

【関東 vs 関西】食文化の違い10選。うなぎ、卵焼き、食パン……。
　　https://www.inshokuten.com/foodist/article/2797/（2020/5/1閲覧）

関東と関西の違いのまとめ　https://jpnculture.net/kanto-kansai-chigai/（2020/6/1閲覧）

北前船とは（北前船寄港地・船主集落）　https://www.kitamae-bune.com/about/main/（2020/5/1閲覧）

キッコーマンホームページ
　　https://www.kikkoman.co.jp/soyworld/museum/index.html（2020/5/1閲覧）

超不思議な関東と関西の違い15選【食文化編】（大日本観光新聞）
　　https://bjtp.tokyo/kanto-kansai-chigai-foods/（2020/5/1閲覧）

第3章／Chapter3

太田静行　『だし・エキスの知識』幸書房　1996

藤村和夫　『だしの本』ハート出版　1997

宮下章　『鰹節（かつおぶし）』（ものと人間の文化史）　法政大学出版局　2000

味の素株式会社　ホームページ　https://www.ajinomoto.co.jp/?scid=av_ot_pc_cojphead_home（2020/5/1閲覧）

にんべんホームページ　https://www.ninben.co.jp（2020/5/1閲覧）

第4章／Chapter4

石毛直道　ケネス・ラドル　『魚醤とナレズシの研究』岩波書店　1990

篠田統　『すしの本』　柴田書店　1966　←初版　現在は岩波現代文庫

藤原昌高　『すし図鑑』　マイナビ出版　2013

『寿司の教科書』e-Mook 宝島社　2013

元禄寿司　回転寿司の歴史　http://www.mawaru-genrokuzusi.co.jp/history/（2020/5/1閲覧）

Mizkan すしラボ

　　http://www.mizkan.co.jp/sushilab/?utm_source=tpb&utm_medium=tpbanner（2020/5/1閲覧）

第5章／Chapter5

岡田哲　『明治洋食事始め　とんかつの誕生』講談社学術文庫　2012

『とんかつフライ料理―人気店のメニューと調理技術』ムック　旭屋出版MOOK　2009

S&B カレー.COM　https://www.sbcurry.com/faq/faq-463/（1/1/2021閲覧）

全日本カレー工業協同組合　http://www.curry.or.jp/whats/number.html（1/1/2021閲覧）

第6章／Chapter6

宮崎正勝　『知っておきたい「食」の日本史』　角川ソフィア文庫　2009

農林水産省　日本の食料自給率（2019）

　　https://www.maff.go.jp/j/zyukyu/zikyu_ritu/attach/pdf/012-16.pdf

第7章／Chapter7

向井由紀子＆橋本慶子『箸（はし）』（ものと人間の文化史）　法政大学出版局　2001

エドワード・ワン　『箸はすごい』　柏書房　2016

第8章／Chapter8

新島繁『蕎麦の事典』（講談社学術文庫）講談社　2011

俣野敏子『そば学大全 日本と世界のソバ食文化』平凡社新書　2002

第9章／Chapter9

小林しのぶ　林　順信『駅弁学講座』集英社新書　2000

MAA(櫻木真奈美)『必ずかわいく作れる キャラ弁の教科書 ― はじめてでもカンタン！』（暮らしニスタ BOOKS）　主婦の友社　2017

山崎和代『はじめてでも作れる！キャラ弁教室』（エイムック 3287）ムック　エイ出版社　2016

駅弁のホームページ　日本鉄道構内営業中央会　http://www.ekiben.or.jp/main/（5/10/2019 閲覧）

【2020】全国の駅弁ランキングTOP21 ！

　　https://travel-noted.jp/posts/29557#head-04197f536208831b5b4657de88c81e98 （12/1/2020閲覧）

第10章／Chapter10

佐々木十美　『日本一の給食：「すべては子どものために」おいしさと安心を追求する"給食の母"の話』学研プラス　2013

藤原辰史　『給食の歴史』　岩波新書　2018

安井孝　『地産地消と学校給食―有機農業と食育のまちづくり』（有機農業選書）　コモンズ　2010

第11章／Chapter11

郷土料理百選(農林水産省選定)　http://www.location-research.co.jp/kyoudoryouri100/ （12/1/2020閲覧）

郷土料理百選パンフレット（農林水産省）

　　https://www.maff.go.jp/j/nousin/kouryu/kyodo_ryouri/panf.html （1/20/2021閲覧）

日本のB級グルメ・ご当地グルメ（JAPAN WEB MAGAZINE）

　　https://japan-web-magazine.com/japanese/food/index/1.html （1/20/2021閲覧）

第12章／Chapter12

青木ゆり子『世界の郷土料理事典：全世界各国・300地域 料理の作り方を通して知る歴史、文化、宗教の食規定』 誠文堂新光社 2020

デイビッド・ウォルトナー＝テーブズ『昆虫食と文明─昆虫の新たな役割を考える』 築地書館 2019

蒲原聖可 『ベジタリアンの医学』(平凡社新書) 平凡社 2005

フレデリック・J. シムーンズ 『肉食タブーの世界史 』(叢書・ウニベルシタス) 法政大学出版局 2001

一般社団法人日本捕鯨協会 https://www.whaling.jp/history.html （1/20/2021閲覧）

International Whaling Commission https://iwc.int/home （1/20/2021閲覧）

コーシャジャパン https://www.kosherjapan.co.jp （1/20/2021閲覧）

世界料理マップ https://e-food.jp/map/ （1/20/2021閲覧）

「多様な食文化・食習慣を有する外国人客への対応マニュアル」(国土交通省観光庁)
　　https://www.mlit.go.jp/kankocho/shisaku/sangyou/taiou_manual.html （1/20/2021閲覧）

ハラル・ジャパン協会 https://jhba.jp （1/20/2021閲覧）

第13章／Chapter13

岡田哲 『ラーメンの誕生』(ちくま学芸文庫) 2019

奥村彪生＆安藤百福『麺の歴史 ラーメンはどこから来たか』(角川ソフィア文庫) 2017

バラク・クシュナー 『ラーメンの歴史学──ホットな国民食からクールな世界食へ』 明石書店 2018

第14章／Chapter14

一島英治 『万葉集にみる食の文化─五穀・菜・塩─』 裳華房 1993

塚本勝巳 『うなぎ 一億年の謎を追う』学研プラス 2014

筒井功 『ウナギと日本人："白いダイヤ"のむかしと今』河出書房新社 2014

ウナギの市場の動態：東アジアにおける生産・取引・消費の分析 (TRAFFIC REPORT) 世界自然保護基金 (WWF)
　　https://www.wwf.or.jp/activities/data/15_Eel_Market_Dynamics_JP.pdf （1/20/2021閲覧）

都道府県別うなぎのかば焼き消費量 https://todo-ran.com/t/kiji/24480 （1/20/2021閲覧）

第15章／Chapter15

葛飾北斎 『北斎漫画 (全)：全15シリーズ完全収録版 (約4000図！)』Kindle Edition 2018

江戸歴史ライブラリー編集部 (編集) 2018

近代食文化研究会 『お好み焼きの戦前史』第二版 2018

那須正幹 『広島お好み物語─ふしぎな食べものが生まれたのはなぜ?』PHP研究所 2004

オタフクソース株式会社 ホームページ https://www.otafuku.co.jp （1/20/2021閲覧）

製粉協会 ホームページ http://www.seifunky.jp （1/20/2021閲覧）

日本コナモン協会 ホームページ http://konamon.com （6/1/2020 閲覧）

著者紹介

畑佐一味・はたさかずみ (Kazumi Hatasa)〔主に本文担当〕

パデュー大学言語文化学科教授

1989 年イリノイ州立大学 Ph.D. 取得 (教育学)。インディアナ州立パデュー大学外国語学科助教授、モナシュ大学准教授を経て現在に到る。2005 年～ 2018 年ミドルベリー大学夏期日本語学校ディレクター。

著書:『なかま 1』『なかま 2』(畑佐由紀子・牧野成一と共著 /Cengage Learning/2014/2018)、『日本語教師のための IT リテラシー』(くろしお出版 /2002)、『第二言語習得研究と言語教育』(畑佐由紀子・百済正和・清水崇文と共編著) / くろしお出版 /2012)

▶1956 年生まれ。東京都出身。落語・小噺と日本語教育での利用、原爆被爆者と海外での証言活動、東日本大震災ドキュメンタリー映画「きょうを守る」の多言語字幕活動、バーチャル・リアリティの日本語教育での可能性、日本の食文化をテーマにした授業など近年の活動範囲は多岐に渡る。

福留奈美・ふくとめなみ (Nami Fukutome)〔主にレシピ担当〕

東京聖栄大学健康栄養学部准教授

2012 年お茶の水女子大学大学院にて博士（学術）取得。専門分野は調理学。2020 年早稲田大学大学院日本語教育研究科修士課程修了。フードコーディネーター、大学・短大・調理師専門学校などの非常勤講師を経て、現在に至る。

著書:『五感で楽しむ食の日本語』(ポリーザトラウスキー編 / くろしお出版 /2021)、『伝え継ぐ 日本の家庭料理』(日本調理科学会企画・編集 / 農山漁村文化協会 /2018-2021)、『和食手帖』(和食文化国民会議監修 /2018)（以上分担執筆）など。

▶1967 年生まれ。高知県出身。調理操作・条件を表す用語・表現研究、食感オノマトペなどのおいしさ表現研究、和菓子の菓銘や料理名・食材名の命名研究など、日本の食文化、調理文化と日本語・日本語教育をつなぐ研究領域を開拓中。和食文化の保護・継承をライフワークとして、食育・味覚教育の講演や執筆活動に取り組む。

【英語翻訳】高頭ルーシー (Lucy Takato)：フリーランス日英翻訳家（料理、食品関係専門）、
NAATI 認定
【装丁デザイン】鈴木章宏
【レシピ写真】亀井宏昭
【写真協力】写真 AC、iStock、やまがたの広報写真ライブラリー、鹿沼市立東中学校、鮨 一新（浅草）

めしあがれ 食文化で学ぶ上級日本語
MESHIAGARE A Culinary Journey through Advanced Japanese

2021年5月25日 第1刷

著者 ● 畑佐一味 福留奈美
発行人 ● 岡野秀夫
発行所 ● くろしお出版
〒102-0084 東京都千代田区二番町4-3
Tel 03-6261-2867 Fax 03-6261-2879
URL http://www.9640.jp Mail kurosio@9640.jp
印刷 ● 亜細亜印刷

© HATASA Kazumi, FUKUTOME Nami 2021, Printed in Japan
ISBN978-4-87424-862-1 C2081